1148525

P9-APM-431

Teaching Kids to CHANGE THE WORLD

LESSONS TO INSPIRE SOCIAL RESPONSIBILITY FOR GRADES 6-12

JENNIFER GRIFFIN-WIESNER, M.Ed.
CHRIS MASER, M.S.

WITHDRAWN

MONTGOMERY COUNTY PUBLIC SCHOOLS
PROFESSIONAL LIBRARY
850 HUNGERFORD DRIVE
ROCKVILLE, MARYLAND 20850

FEB 1 3 2008

SEARCH
INSTITUTE
PRESS

Teaching Kids to Change the World:
Lessons to Inspire Social Responsibility for Grades 6–12

The following are registered trademarks of Search
Institute: Search Institute® and Developmental Assets®.

Jennifer Griffin-Wiesner, M.Ed., and Chris Maser, M.S.

Search Institute Press, Minneapolis, MN
Copyright © 2008 by Search Institute

All rights reserved. No part of this publication may be
reproduced in any manner, mechanical or electronic,
without prior permission from the publisher except in
brief quotations or summaries in articles or reviews, or
as individual activity sheets for educational use only. For
additional permission, write to Permissions at Search
Institute.

At the time of publication, all facts and figures cited herein
are the most current available; all telephone numbers,
addresses, and Web site URLs are accurate and active; all
publications, organizations, Web sites, and other resources
exist as described in this book; and all efforts have been
made to verify them. The author and Search Institute make
no warranty or guarantee concerning the information and
materials given out by organizations or content found at
Web sites that are cited herein, and we are not responsible
for any changes that occur after this book's publication. If
you find an error or believe that a resource listed herein is
not as described, please contact Client Services at Search
Institute.

10 9 8 7 6 5 4 3 2 1
Printed on acid-free paper in the United States of America.

Search Institute
615 First Avenue Northeast, Suite 125
Minneapolis, MN 55413
www.search-institute.org
612-376-8955 · 800-888-7828

ISBN-13: 978-1-57482-877-1
ISBN-10: 1-57482-877-0

Library of Congress Cataloging-in-Publication Data
Griffin-Wiesner, Jennifer.
    Teaching kids to change the world : lessons to inspire
    social responsibility for grades 6–12 / Jennifer Griffin-
    Wiesner and Chris Maser.
        p. cm.
    Includes bibliographical references.
    ISBN-13: 978-1-57482-877-1 (pbk. : alk. paper)
    ISBN-10: 1-57482-877-0 (pbk. : alk. paper)
    1. Citizenship--Study and teaching (Elementary)
    2. Creative activities and seat work.
        I. Maser, Chris. II. Title.
    LC1091.G74 2008
    370.11'5--dc22
                    2007037308

Credits
Editors: Tenessa Gemelke, Susan Wootten
Book Design: Jeenee Lee
Production Coordinator: Mary Ellen Buscher

Permissions
Grateful acknowledgment is made to the Southern Poverty
Law Center for permission to adapt "Classroom Utopia"
from its Teaching Tolerance website at www.tolerance.org.

About Search Institute Press
Search Institute Press is a division of Search Institute, a
nonprofit organization that offers leadership, knowledge,
and resources to promote positive youth development. Our
mission at Search Institute Press is to provide practical
and hope-filled resources to help create a world in which
all young people thrive. Our products are embedded in
research and the 40 Developmental Assets—qualities,
experiences, and relationships youth need to succeed—are
a central focus of our resources. Our logo, the SIP flower, is
a symbol of the thriving and healthy growth young people
experience when they have an abundance of assets in
their lives.

Licensing and Copyright
The educational activity sheets in *Teaching Kids to Change
the World: Lessons to Inspire Social Responsibility for Grades
6–12* may be copied as needed. For each copy, please
respect the following guidelines: Do not remove, alter,
or obscure the Search Institute credit and copyright
information on any activity sheet. Clearly differentiate
any material you add for local distribution from material
prepared by Search Institute. Do not alter the Search
Institute material in content or meaning. Do not resell the
activity sheets for profit. Include the following attribution
when you use the information from the activity sheets in
other formats for promotional or educational purposes:
**Reprinted with permission from *Teaching Kids to Change
the World: Lessons to Inspire Social Responsibility for Grades
6–12* (title of activity sheet). Copyright © 2008 by Search
Institute, 800-888-7828, www.search-institute.org.
All rights reserved.**

Printing Tips
To produce high-quality copies of activity sheets for
distribution without spending a lot of money, follow
these tips: Always copy from the original; copying from a
copy lowers the reproduction quality. Make copies more
appealing by using brightly colored paper or even colored
ink. Quick-print shops often run daily specials on certain
colors of ink. For variety, consider printing each activity
sheet on a different color of paper. If you are using more
than one activity sheet or an activity sheet that runs
more than one page, make two-sided copies. Use at least
60-pound offset paper so that the words don't bleed
through, as often happens with 20-pound paper.

For our beloved change agents, Isaac & Nora Griffin-Wiesner
and Linus & Friday Gemelke Lee

Contents

Preface

If you understand, things are just as they are . . .
If you do not understand, things are just as they are.
Zen proverb

"Teaching kids to change the world" sounds like a lofty ambition; we recognize that. But change happens all around us, every day, whether or not we do anything about it. Thus, we have a choice: we can "become the change [we] want to see in the world" (as Mohandas K. Gandhi encouraged), or we can simply react to change as it occurs.

Everything—living creatures, plants, air, water, inanimate objects, time and space, everything—exists in relationship to everything else. Each action you and your students take is like a pebble dropped into a quiet pool of water. Just as each pebble produces a unique set of ripples—a series of changes—so does each child and adult offer a unique gift to the world.

Each gift is different and valuable in its service to the earth and its inhabitants. And what is true of individual humans is also true for all cultures and societies. No matter how strongly we strive for autonomy, each life, culture, and society is interdependent. Each also has its own excellence and cannot be justly compared to another.

A pebble's impact on the water's surface creates concentric rings flowing outward from the center, touching everything in their path. The farther the rings travel from the epicenter, the wider and more diffuse they become. Sharp eyes might catch their visual disappearance, but no witness will observe their ultimate dissipation because the rings continue to exist in every other thing they have touched.

Imagine, for a moment, a young child sitting by a pond at the edge of a meadow:

A spider, carrying her silken case full of eggs, walks across the surface of the water. To see how fast she can run, the child tosses a pebble into the pond. Startled by the impact of the pebble as it strikes the surface, the spider runs to safety at the pool's edge, only to be eaten by a pregnant frog. Some of the atoms that once composed the spider and her eggs now become part of the frog's body, and thus part of the frog's eggs as well.

When the frog's eggs hatch, a bit of the spider and her babies lives on in each tadpole. Inevitably, some of the tadpoles will die, and the atoms they acquired from the spider and her eggs now become part of the grass growing along the water's edge. The grass, in turn, is eaten by a meadow mouse, which is eaten by a snake that is itself eaten by a hawk. Other atoms from the spider and her babies hop away in the form of frogs that have metamorphosed from surviving tadpoles, on their way to participate in the perpetual progression of life.

The hawk hunts in a nearby forest, where it kills and eats a mother warbler on her way to feed her young. When the mother does not return, hunger drives the largest of the babies to abandon its siblings and hunt for food on the limb supporting the nest. There it finds spiders and ants to eat, and thus survives until it can fly.

With the passing of summer, the young warbler matures and migrates south, taking with it an atom from the fallen, rotten, ancient fir tree in which its mother nested.

While wintering in South America, the warbler dies and falls into a jungle stream, where a scavenging fish eats it. The fish will be caught, cooked, and eaten by the son of a subsistence farmer. A year later, the boy will leave his jungle home to attend school in the city.

After some years, the boy will go to sea as a merchant seaman and die an old man on a distant shore, where the atom of the ancient tree (once a part of the mother warbler's migrating offspring, who became part of the fish that became part of the boy) will enter yet another strand of life's web.

Meanwhile, miles from the pool, a spider builds its web along the edge of the forest bordering a farmer's field. A fly becomes entangled in the web. The spider eats the fly. A passing sparrow eats the spider. The hunting hawk—which ate the snake, the mouse (which ate the grass by the edge of the pool), and the mother warbler—now chases the sparrow, which flies toward the farmyard for safety.

The farmer, assuming all hawks are hunting his prize chickens, shoots the hawk. Seeing the hawk plummet from the sky, the farmer walks back to his barn to put away his shotgun, where he trips and falls, driving a rusty nail into his hand. Giving little thought to the wound, the farmer continues his daily routine, unaware that he has contracted the tetanus that leads to his death.

What might have happened had the spider constructed its web elsewhere? Would the fly still have been caught? Suppose the fly had avoided the web or become entangled at a different time? Would the spider's activity have attracted the sparrow, which attracted the hawk that chased it? Had the chase occurred a few minutes earlier (or later), would the farmer have seen the hawk or decided to shoot it? Without a reason to hoist his gun, the farmer might not later have tripped and fallen in the barn, and would not have set in motion the events that led to his infection and eventual death.

For an instant in time, the atoms that compose a living being continue their journey as they participate in and create a perpetually widening series of stories about eternal relationships within the one story. And that one story, like the spider's silken case of eggs—and like your group of students—contains all the other stories.

Whatever we do is part of a tale that reverberates throughout eternity. Just as no pebble can strike the water's surface without causing an effect, no action can exist without a cause.

This universal truth is the essence—the heart—of the power and wonder of being a teacher, and it is why we wrote this book. You are, in many ways, serving as your students' muse, providing the context, skills, and inspiration they will use to craft their own story line. As an educator and youth leader, in a formal or informal setting, your influence on young people is often second only to that of their families. You are in a remarkable position to show young people how they can be powerful, positive agents of change throughout their lives. In *Teaching Kids to Change the World*, we share with you stories from our many years of working to help people of all ages empower themselves to change the world for the better.

Introduction: We Have a Choice

History teaches us that men and nations behave wisely
once they have exhausted all other alternatives.
Abba Eban (1915–2002), Israeli diplomat and politician

We are intrigued by the Zen concept of a beginner's mind—a mind that is still open to the dance of imagination in the land of innocence and possibility. This dance is one that most adults must work hard to retain in a world that values the pursuit of concrete knowledge. Far too many of us forget our unique, childlike ability to ask, "Why?"

In our work with young people, we've observed that around the time children enter grade 4, adults begin to instill in them a focus on what to think, rather than on how to think. We consider a three-year-old's "Why?" to be charming and developmentally appropriate, but all too often a 10-year-old's "Why?" is met with "That's just how it is."

As early as 1933, the conservationist and author Aldo Leopold put his finger on the beginnings of this trend when he wrote, "To build a better motor we tap the uttermost powers of the human brain; to build a better countryside we throw dice." And while adults continue creating social and environmental problems (Aldo Leopold's dice throwing), these same young people will be asked to solve those problems because we adults are increasingly incapable of doing so ourselves.

Without the knowledge, skills, and competencies to creatively deal with social and environmental issues, no society has a viable context within which to greet the children it brings into the world—much less nurture them.

Thus, if we want to change our world for the better, we must tap into the creative and positive energy of young people. Over and over again we've seen that it is the children who teach their parents and other elders about the components of sustainability—not the other way around. The middle school and high school years present a critical developmental opportunity, because well into adolescence and early adulthood, the neural connections of young people's brains are literally being "hardwired" in terms of how youth think about themselves, their relationships, their choices, and their decisions.

CHANGE BEGINS WITH YOU

This book is for those of you—whether educators, youth leaders, or other types of story weavers—who are committed to giving young people a strong, powerful, positive voice—a voice that is robust and hopeful enough to rally kindred spirits of all ages. This commitment makes you unique and critical to the sustainability of our planet.

Adults are the trustees of young people's futures. Yet we rarely ask young people what we should leave as our legacy, nor do we always listen when they try to share their ideas about real-life issues. Why? Because, collectively, we are too busy to attend to young people's intuitive wisdom—which we also once had as children, but have since lost in today's competitive "hurry, worry" world of materialism, clashing ideologies, and attempts to control circumstances. The notion of fairness and human dignity, however, demands of us one of our scarcest resources—our willingness to listen to one another. Not listening invalidates the feelings, the very existence, of another person—an all-too-frequent occurrence experienced by young people.

Our children will one day become local, national, and international leaders. Many of us may still be around when that time comes. The better our young people are at finding positive, creative, sustainable ways of working, playing, and being together, the more they will be able to truly change the world.

ABOUT THIS BOOK

Teaching Kids to Change the World centers on eight principles of change that feature adaptable, easy-to-use lessons. The **lessons** include stories and examples illustrating a principle's main points and help you engage young people in learning about their influence on the people, creatures, and environments that surround them. We suggest ways to teach young people how to apply their learning to the choices they make every day—from the products they buy to the food they eat to the transportation they use, and beyond.

Each **principle** contains elements of one or more of the following subjects: sociology, ecology, biology, environmental studies, oral and written communication, peaceful conflict resolution, physics, chemistry, and personal growth and development. At the conclusion of each principle, we identify suggestions for putting **lessons** into action beyond the classroom. Basic information and concepts are presented with options for adding complexity to better meet your students' needs. In some cases, we share **real-life examples** from our own experience that particularly highlight the principle at hand. We encourage you to read these and, if appropriate, summarize them for your students as a way of making real-life applications to the teachings. Better yet, allow your students to spark your own memories of lessons learned and wisdom acquired, which you can pass on to them.

Activities included with each lesson focus on helping young people understand social responsibility—specifically, the notion that the choices people make every day will have long-lasting implications for present and future physical and social environments.

Before you dive headlong into the eight principles, it's important to understand a fundamental approach to positive thinking that may be new and different for your students (and perhaps for you). A number of years ago, Search Institute, a Minnesota-based nonprofit education research organization, discovered the power of emphasizing the promise and potential within each individual young person. Using the *Search Institute Profiles of Student Life: Attitudes and Behaviors* survey, the institute's researchers measured adolescent behaviors through a positive lens, asking young people about the strengths and supports in their lives, rather than focusing solely on the struggles and challenges they faced.

Response to the survey findings, from adults and young people alike, was unprecedented. Eventually, the survey resulted in the Developmental Assets framework (see page 73 for a complete list), which provides a positive foundation upon which to nurture healthy, productive, and involved young people.

This book is organized around principles of social responsibility through which you can empower young people to take ownership of their world and create an environment that nurtures assets. The Developmental Assets framework allows you to help young people view the world through the lens of their own strengths (upon which other strengths can be built), rather than simply overwhelming them with a litany of problems they must overcome.

Principles of Social Responsibility

1. Life Is an Open-Ended Experiment

2. Everything We Do Is an Exercise in Relationships

3. Change Is a Universal Constant

4. Act Locally and Affect the Whole World

5. Ecology and Economy Are Each One Half of the House We Live In

6. Relationships, Not Numbers, Keep Systems Sustainable

7. We Can Only Manage Ourselves

8. True Sustainability Requires a Shared Vision

Life Is an Open-Ended Experiment

Security is mostly a superstition. It does not exist in Nature. . . .
Life is either a daring adventure or nothing.

Helen Keller (1880–1968), American activist and author

The realities we accept as obvious, neutral, objective, and simply "the way the world works" are actually structures we create as we think and live. They are created by our rendition of history, our understanding of ourselves, of society, and of our world—and they are a partial view of the whole. Our individual knowledge is always limited, and we must be mindful of our own naïveté.

LESSON 1

It Is Wise to Have a Beginner's Mind

Several years ago, Jennifer and her husband, John, traveled with friends and family to Castlegregory, Ireland. One of the natural highlights of this lush area is Inch Strand, a long, wide stretch of light sand and blue-green water. At low tide the beach expands up to an additional mile, leaving plenty of room for exploration.

In addition to its natural beauty, the beach has a rich history. The remains of Ireland's oldest civilization were excavated from dunes behind the strand. Pirates reportedly lured ships onto the sands in bad weather and then plundered them. More recently, several films have been produced here.

During their holiday, Jennifer and John borrowed a rental car from their traveling companions. Their first ill-advised decision was to drive a rental car for which they were not insured. After a bit of shopping they headed to the strand.

The beach was longer and lovelier than words can describe and seemed to melt into the ocean at its tip. John really wanted to see the tip. That's when they made their second bad decision. Despite the large "Do NOT Drive on the Strand" sign, they drove onto the beach.

Flying along in the car, the strand felt

light and smooth, which led John to comment that he couldn't see what the problem was; driving on the sand, he observed, was much like driving in snow, as he and Jennifer had so often and capably done at home in Minnesota. In fact, like many native Minnesotans, they prided themselves on being experts when it came to driving in snow.

Then they stopped—their third bad decision.

Once stopped, they could not get going again. The car's wheels simply spun deeper into the soft sand, encountering more and more of it. It did feel like being stuck in snow, although with snow one eventually hits frozen ground or road. On a beach, of course, the tide eventually rolls in. For a while, John and Jennifer just stood and watched, not knowing what else to do.

Finally, three kind souls stopped to help. After many unsuccessful attempts by John to drive while the others pushed, one of the Irish gentlemen—bemused but also familiar with this type of situation—told John to get out of the car. With four people pushing, he slipped the car into second gear and shot off down the beach—with the car, Jennifer and John's passports, gifts in the trunk, and some of their money. Their rental cottage had no phone, and Inch Strand was several miles from the nearest town.

Fortunately, this story has a happy ending. The man drove all the way to the warning sign (perhaps to emphasize the travelers' flagrant disregard for local regulations), and stopped there to wait for them. John and Jennifer didn't speak on the entire drive back to Castlegregory. They have never again been foolish enough to think they could outsmart nature and the collective wisdom of a local culture.

Because Jennifer and John considered themselves expert drivers, they thought they knew better than the local people what they could do on the beach with a vehicle—based solely on the appearance of the beach and their experience driving in snow. Such thinking blinded them to what they didn't know about the differences between a snowy road and a sandy beach.

If we believe we are always experts, then we often think we know what the answers should be (that driving on a snowy road and a sandy beach are interchangeable circumstances requiring the same skills), but the reality is that we can no longer see all of what the answers might be. A beginner, on the other hand, is free to explore and discover a multiplicity of realities (often thought of as "beginner's luck"), while the expert grows rigid in a self-created box composed of a single reality. The beginner thus may understand a question better than the expert, and is less likely to become literally or figuratively stuck in solving a problem. Children, with their intuitive wisdom, often understand this concept better than adults.

ACTIVITY

FLIP THE ISLAND

Purpose

To illustrate for young people that being open to figuring something out, even if the task seems difficult or impossible, often sparks tremendous creativity and problem solving.

Materials

A large tarp or sheet (about 5 feet by 5 feet)

Class Steps

1. Tell the class that the tarp or sheet represents an island.
2. Say that a group from the class is going to go camping on the island. Ask for five or six volunteers to step onto the island.
3. Then say: "I forgot to mention that the campsite needs to be rotated in order to conserve the area." Since it's so small, the only option is to flip the tarp over.
4. Instruct the group to flip over the tarp without stepping or falling into the

shark-infested "water" all around.

5. If necessary, tell the group they must not lift anyone above shoulder level.

6. When the tarp has been successfully turned over, ask for five or six new volunteers and repeat the process until all students have had a chance to participate.

Follow-up Discussion

1. What did you think of the task when it was first described? Did it seem possible? Why or why not?

2. Describe how you figured out a solution for flipping the tarp.

3. How did the first group approach the exercise? Later groups?

4. Did you "know" intuitively what to do?

5. Did you have ideas you thought might work? What were they? Did they work the way you thought they would?

6. When you were a spectator, did you think the group standing on the island would be able to flip it? Why or why not?

TAKING IT TO THE NEXT LEVEL

LIFE IS AN OPEN-ENDED EXPERIMENT

Throughout *Teaching Kids to Change the World*, we provide suggestions for taking concepts "to the next level" and helping young people have beginners' minds regarding their abilities to find, explore, and try new and different ways to change the world. Start with the activities below to encourage young people to think in new ways about themselves and their lives.

Level 1

Explain to students that one part of who they are is how they spend their time. We each have 24 hours a day to spend on fun, work, learning, chores, and taking care of ourselves. Ask students to sketch a clock face on paper and write on it or decorate it with the ways they spend an average day. They can illustrate a typical school day, a weekend, or both. After the clocks are completed, hold a group discussion about what students learned, any surprises they encountered, and what, if anything, they might like to change.

Level 2

Distribute copies of *Resource 1: Finding a Path to Explore* on page 4. Ask students to read through the information and add ideas of their own.

Level 3

Talk with students about how acting according to their beliefs is often not as simple as they might think. Questions that seem at first to have clear "black and white" answers may later appear in shades of gray when it comes time to make a choice. Use *Resource 2: Black, White, and Gray* on page 5 as a discussion starter.

Finding a Path to Explore

Look through the list of real-life situations below. Circle the ones you might want to experience. Then scan the chart to see how certain skills, classes, and experiences can help you get there. Be sure to add your own ideas as well.

EXPERIENCES I MIGHT WANT TO TRY	WHAT I NEED TO KNOW	WAYS I COULD LEARN MORE
Going to trade school, community college, or university	• What I like to do • What I'm good at • What kinds of schools are available and what their costs are • How to complete admissions and loan applications _____ _____	• Ask adults who have interesting jobs to let me "shadow" them for a day • Join clubs to find out what interests me • Get help from a librarian or school counselor in finding out about schools _____ _____
Performing my own songs with my own band	• How to write poetry and song lyrics • How to play an instrument • What different music styles are like • What it takes to promote a band _____ _____	• Take writing and music classes • Join a school or community music group • Listen to a variety of radio stations • Work as an intern at a radio station • Work in a music store _____ _____
Traveling outside the country	• What type of transportation and travel documents I'll need • Where I can find maps of places I want to visit • Where I might stay • What requirements I need to meet to enter another country • How much I'll need to budget for my trip • How to communicate in another language _____ _____	• Use the Internet and library to find information • Visit the post office for information on passports • Talk to people who have traveled to places I'd like to visit • Take language classes and use Internet language-teaching sites • Visit embassy Web sites for health and visa information _____ _____

Adapted with permission from *Take It to the Next Level* by Kathryn L. Hong (Search Institute, 2004). From *Teaching Kids to Change the World: Lessons to Inspire Social Responsibility for Grades 6–12* by Jennifer Griffin-Wiesner, M.Ed., and Chris Maser, M.S. This page may be reproduced for educational, noncommercial uses only. Copyright © 2008 by Search Institute; 800-888-7828; www.search-institute.org.

Black, White, and Gray

Acting according to your beliefs is often not as simple as it sounds. Questions that first seem to have "black and white" answers may later appear in shades of gray when it comes time to make a choice. Think about the following scenes—what would you do?

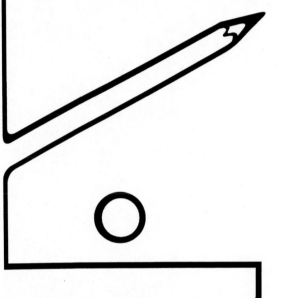

Scene 1

Your friend writes a poem. She asks you to read it and tell her what you honestly think of it.

1. What would your "black and white" answer be? Why?

2. Suppose it's your friend's first poem, and you don't want to discourage her from trying again—what would you say?

3. What would you say if you don't know much about the kind of effort it takes to write a good poem?

Scene 2

Math is a subject that comes easily to you. One of your friends asks you to do his math homework for him.

1. What would your "black and white" answer be? Why?

2. What if your friend just doesn't seem able to understand the math homework, no matter how hard he tries?

3. What would you say if your friend is failing math and is in danger of being kicked off the soccer team if he fails the assignment?

Scene 3

You have a boyfriend or girlfriend whom you really care about. That person is pushing you to be more physically intimate than is comfortable for you.

1. What would your "black and white" answer be? Why?

2. What would you say if your boyfriend or girlfriend tells you that if you are really in love, you'll do what he or she wants you to do?

3. What would you say if you've promised your parents or yourself that you will wait for more physical intimacy until you're older and/or you're married?

Adapted with permission from *Take It to the Next Level* by Kathryn L. Hong (Search Institute, 2004). From *Teaching Kids to Change the World: Lessons to Inspire Social Responsibility for Grades 6–12* by Jennifer Griffin-Wiesner, M.Ed., and Chris Maser, M.S. This page may be reproduced for educational, noncommercial uses only. Copyright © 2008 by Search Institute; 800-888-7828; www.search-institute.org.

Everything We Do Is an Exercise in Relationships

The future belongs to those who believe in the beauty of their dreams.

Eleanor Roosevelt (1884–1962), American political leader

Nothing can exist outside the context of a relationship. Everything you do, therefore, is an exercise in relationship, just as you experience a relationship with gravity when you pick up this book (if you release the book, it will fall). Further, you are practicing a relationship with the cloud that brought the rain that nurtured the tree that was cut and hauled to the paper mill, where it was prepared as pulp to make the paper upon which these words are printed.

When you read these words, you are practicing a relationship with the meaning stored in them through written language—the archive of humanity's journey through time. And you might explain this idea to your students through the spoken word, which holds the same meaning as the written word, stored in sound, with which you are also practicing a relationship.

LESSON 2

Everything Is Defined by Relationships

Try as we might to control our physical surroundings, our day-to-day experiences, and our "inputs and outputs," our relationships to these things are constantly changing. Hence, there is no such thing in our environment as an independent variable or a constant value.

The first time our friend Ann visited the Nicoya Peninsula of Costa Rica, she was delighted to see and hear the many howler monkeys living in the area. Ann, a Midwesterner, thought the monkeys were both exotic and exciting. When she and her family moved to Costa Rica several years later, they were delighted to find many monkeys living on their property. However, the longer Ann and her family lived in Costa Rica, the less enchanted they felt, as their relationship with the monkeys began to change.

In fact, the monkeys became a nuisance, especially when their loud howling pierced the early morning calm. After all, the monkeys are called "howlers" for a good reason—although they sound less like howling dogs or wolves than they do screeching airplanes landing or large pieces of machinery rolling in. Regardless of how you might interpret the sound, it seems to come from everywhere at once.

Next, something happened to further change the family's relationship with the monkeys. A baby howler, which normally rode on its mother's back, fell from the trees into Ann's yard. The family dog, Luna, whom they had adopted in part as protection from wild animals entering their home, found the baby monkey and began carrying it around—perhaps to play with or eat.

Ann and her 10-year-old son became concerned about the young monkey's safety, as did its mother, who was waiting in a nearby tree. After a good deal of coaxing, Ann eventually convinced Luna to release the baby howler and come back to the house.

At first the monkey lay completely still on the ground, at some distance from the tree. After several moments it lifted its head and slowly pulled itself closer to its mother. Several more minutes passed, and it did the same thing again. This time, the baby monkey's mother was able to reach down and retrieve her baby, after which she scampered off, with her baby riding "monkey back."

In a relatively short time, Ann and her family experienced the howler monkeys as an exotic treat, a thrill, a nuisance, as mother and child, as chew toy, as a victim, and as a survivor.

ACTIVITY
GARBLED MARBLES

Purpose
To demonstrate that, while the physical characteristics of marbles (such as size and weight) do not change, the way they behave and relate to one another changes significantly as their environment (or context) changes.

Materials
- Flat aluminum pie pan
- Slightly dented aluminum pie pan
- Ten marbles of the same size
- Two or three marbles of different sizes
- Paper and pen

Class Steps
1. Place the flat pan on a level tabletop.
2. Put ten same-size marbles in the pan any way you wish. Observe how they are spaced in relation to one another and to the edge of the pan.
3. Move one marble. How does it appear in relation to its neighbors and to the edge of the pan—closer? Farther away?
4. Take one marble out of the pan. Does removing one marble affect the other nine marbles? If so, how?
5. Now, replace the marble and add an odd-sized marble. Has this addition affected the others in the pan? If so, how?
6. Transfer the marbles to the slightly dented pan. How does the placement (relationship) of the marbles change in the pan? What happens if the pan and marbles are placed on a slant? How does this change affect their relationship?

Note: If students don't perceive the effects of these steps, point out the way marbles quiver or roll when the conditions are changed.

Follow-up Discussion
1. Is there anything you can do to the marbles in either the flat pan or the bent

pan that will not have an effect on the other marbles or on the pan itself?

2. What does this experiment tell you about how the parts of this experiment relate to one another?

3. What can we learn from this exercise about relationships between other objects? Between plants and animals? Between people?

LESSON 3

All Relationships Have Consequences

While working in Egypt in 1963, Chris decided to visit a black hill in the Egyptian desert about 300 miles southwest of Alexandria. This part of Egypt is flat and sandy, featuring vast areas of desert pavement, which consists of small-ish rocks that cover the surface of the sand.

After traveling by Jeep for some time, Chris's Bedouin guide instructed him (through an interpreter) to steer the Jeep a few inches to the right. To Chris, the instruction sounded ridiculous. He wondered what difference a tiny adjustment of three inches could possibly make in the journey. The man didn't even have a map! Nevertheless, Chris was finally persuaded to make this seemingly insignificant change.

Two days later they arrived at the black hill. The guide told Chris to look at his map of the region. When they spread the map on the hood of the jeep, Chris learned a lesson in humility. His guide drew a triangle show-ing that the course correction of three inches near Alexandria had saved about 50 miles on the way to the black hill. Had the travel-ers gone Chris' way, they would not have had enough fuel or water for the return trip, which would have resulted in possible dehydration or even death.

Chris learned that the further he made predictions into the trackless future, the more conscious and clear he had to be about:

- Where he wanted to go, and why;
- How he was going to navigate;
- The value of a successful journey; and
- The cost his success would impose on others.

The last condition was of extra importance. Had the group continued Chris's way, they would never have found the black hill, and the bones of three travelers might still be bleach-ing in the desert decades later.

We humans exist in relationship to our surroundings. And it is also the case that every relationship gives us a feeling, a sensa-tion—and that is a consequence. Think for a moment about how you feel and what the sen-sation or consequence is when you experience the following:

- Your students enter your classroom for the first time each day.
- The last student leaves each day.
- You arrive home at day's end.
- You gaze upon a glorious sunrise or sunset.
- You burn yourself on a hot stove.
- You have a flat tire on your way to work.
- You have a serious disagreement with a friend.
- Someone close to you dies.
- You see a loved one after a long absence.
- You discover the first flower of spring.
- You leave on a long-anticipated vacation.

Each of these circumstances evokes a sen-sation, a feeling that epitomizes your relation-ship with a momentary aspect of life, whether you are conscious of it or not. Ultimately, these seemingly isolated incidents coalesce to give you an overall experience of your life as you perceive it. On the other hand, should two people face precisely the same circumstances in their lives, each would experience them differently, because they are different people from different backgrounds, which causes them to perceive the world differently. In the end, life consists of a series of relationships that create other series of relationships, and each encounter results in a consequence.

ACTIVITY
SOMETIMES LITTLE THINGS MEAN A LOT

Purpose
Students experience the significant long-term impact that even seemingly tiny adjustments in their approaches can make.

Materials
- Athletic field
- Tape measure or ruler

Class Steps
1. Starting at the center of an athletic field, divide the class into three groups.
2. From the same starting point, ask all students to face one end of the field. Send the first group walking on a straight line in this direction.
3. Next, have the second group turn slightly to the right and send the second group off on a straight line of travel.
4. Have the third group turn slightly to the left and send this group off on a straight line of travel.

Follow-up Discussion
1. What are the outcomes—the consequences—of these minor "target corrections"?
2. How significant would the correction of a single inch be in the construction of a square, single-story house, a 30-story building, or a mile-long bridge?
3. If you are simply talking with another person, do minor shifts in your posture change the way you can or cannot relate to that person?
4. Can the small changes you make in your life lead to bigger corrections (consequences)? How? Give examples.

LESSON 4
Composition, Structure, and Function Are Intertwined

When is a chair not a chair?

We perceive objects by means of their obvious structures or functions. Composition refers to the elements or parts. Structure, whether simple or complex, is the way those elements are put together, and can be thought of as the overall organization, arrangement, or makeup of a thing. Function, on the other hand, is what a particular structure either can do or allows to be done to or with it.

A chair is a chair because of its structure, which gives it a particular shape. A chair can be characterized as a piece of furniture composed of a seat, four legs, a back, and often arms. Its composition and structure are determined by its function: to accommodate a sitting person. Because of the seat, we can sit in a chair. It's the act of sitting, the functional component allowed by the structure, that makes a chair . . . well . . . a chair.

What happens if we remove the seat? Now in order to sit, you must be seated on the ground between the legs of the "chair." By definition, when we remove a chair's seat, we no longer have a chair, because we have changed the structure by altering its composition, and so we have also altered its function. Thus, the structure of an object defines its function and is dependent upon a necessary composition of parts, and the function of an object dictates a necessary structure.

To maintain ecological functions means that one must maintain the characteristics of the ecosystem in such a way that its processes are sustainable. The characteristics one must be concerned with are:

- *Composition*—Flora, fauna, water sources, soil, and so on;

- *Structure*—The way elements are configured; and
- *Function*—The purpose or role of each element, as well as the ways in which they interact.

Here, composition determines the structure and function. If we change the composition (as with the seat of the aforementioned chair), we simultaneously change both the structure and the function. We can change the composition of an ecosystem, such as the kinds and arrangement of plants within a forest, and we can change the composition of our social environments—schools, neighborhoods, towns and cities—as well.

The kinds of plants within a plant community create a certain structure that is characteristic of that plant community. It's the structure of the plant community that in turn creates and maintains certain functions. In addition, it is the composition, structure, and function of a plant community that determine what kinds of animals can live in a particular location, how many, and for how long—just as the composition and structure of a particular house determine who can live there (a person who earns a modest salary can hardly afford a million-dollar home, and a person who uses a wheelchair would be unlikely to purchase a three-story house with a steep set of stairs).

If we change the composition of a forest, we change its structure and function also, thus affecting animals in the forest, which are ultimately constrained by the forest's composition. Suppose a human community wants a particular animal or group of animals to thrive within its forests (perhaps a rich diversity of summering birds that attract tourist dollars from birdwatchers). Members of the community would work backward from their goal, first determining the function they value.

Function dictates the kind of structure to create, which means knowing the type of composition necessary to produce the required habitat for the animal valued by the commu-

nity. Once the composition is determined, the structure and its accompanying functions operate together in terms of the habitat required for the animals.

People and nature continually change the structure and function of this or that system—whether social or environmental—by manipulating the composition, which subsequently changes the composition of humans and other animals dependent on the structure and function of the resultant habitat.

For example, by altering the composition of plants within an ecosystem, people and nature also alter the structure, which in turn affects how the ecosystem functions, which determines not only the kinds and quantities of animals that can live there, but also the uses we humans can make of the ecosystem. You can help your students develop tremendous personal power and influence by encouraging them to think about how they can change for the better the composition of the environments—the contexts—they seek to improve.

ACTIVITY
IS THE GRASS ALWAYS GREENER?

Purpose
Students see that changing the composition, structure, or function of the water changes the way the grass seed responds.

Materials
- Four large trays with 1- to 2-inch-high sides
- Enough grass seed to cover the bottoms of the trays
- Potting soil
- Three types of water: purified, tap, and water contaminated with some sort of weed killer

Class Steps
1. Following instructions on the seed package, plant an equal amount of grass seed in each of the four trays.

2. Water the grass seed regularly according to instructions, using a different type of water for each of three trays. Do not water the fourth tray.

3. Regularly observe the progress of the grass until it grows to a desired height.

Follow-up Discussion

1. What happened in each of the trays?

2. What does this tell us about how water affects the plants it hydrates? What does that tell us about how our decisions concerning water have effects beyond the water itself?

3. What would happen if, instead of grass growing in trays, these were wild rice plants growing in a stream or marsh? (Wood ducks, muskrats, and white-tailed deer all depend on the rice, as do humans.)

4. What does this tell us about how introducing or removing elements of an ecosystem might change the way the system works?

LESSON 5
Context Affects Relationships

Besides structure and function, our universe contains the characteristic of context—the way in which an object interacts with, or relates to, its environment. The notion of context is important because our thinking, and therefore our view of the world, is generally limited to one piece of the puzzle—our own experience and exposure to particular (and often limited) information.

To examine how a piece relates to the whole, go back to the example of the chair, picturing it in a room. If you stand in the doorway and survey the room, you will see the chair both in the room and in relation to the room: it's in the middle, or in a far corner, or near the door. In contrast, when you focus only on the chair, or go right up to it and examine it closely, you no longer see the room or the chair's place within it.

To illustrate this notion of context and how it affects relationships in a human-centered way, consider the example of a large discount retailer's relationship with a small town.

Suppose a community with a population of 8,000 has two restaurants—a café and a family diner—along with a small clothing store; a pharmacy that sells ice cream, develops photos, and features locally crafted wares; a meat market; a liquor store; two bars; and a small grocery with one gas pump. A large discount retailer opens its doors just outside the town limits. Residents are excited: They can buy—at much lower prices—their household staples in bulk, such as paper products, packaged food items, and other household goods, as well as a wider range of clothing (much of it manufactured outside the country), and a huge selection of gift items. A number of people from the town obtain jobs at the store and meet people from nearby towns who are also employed there.

Inside the store, customers also discover self-service photo developing, a snack counter, great deals on meat and other food items, and a 24-hour pharmacy. They are astounded by the wide selection and enthusiastic about having more consumer choice.

Eventually, the local café, grocery, pharmacy, and meat market experience a drop in sales, but manage to keep their doors open by reducing staff hours. Soon, the discount store adds a liquor outlet, six gas pumps, and a car wash. A popular restaurant chain opens next door. Again, neighbors are enthusiastic about having more dining options, and the discount store becomes more of a destination, especially when a fast-food restaurant joins the mix.

One by one, the small businesses in town begin to fail. Shops close because they can't compete with the prices of their new competitors; the family café and diner find that business slows to a crawl; owners begin to lose money. Some of those who have lost their jobs find new ones at the discount store, but others have to start commuting to more distant jobs or collect unemployment payments. Of those who commute, some relocate. Others find that, despite their resentment of the impact of the discount store, it's now their only shopping option between work and home.

Not so many years after the discount store opens, the only business establishments still open are the local bars. The majority of profits from the discount store go to outside shareholders and executives. Very little of the money being earned by residents is reinvested locally. Most young people leave town to find education and jobs elsewhere. Older people with limited mobility must move to larger towns in order to gain access to the resources and services they need. The community, once a vital, bustling village, now resembles a ghost town.

ACTIVITY

VARIATION ON "MUSICAL CHAIRS"

Purpose
Students experience a change in their view of the chairs as the chairs become scarcer (and thus in higher demand), and see the game in a new way.

Materials
- A chair for each student
- Music source (a radio, CD or tape player)

Preparation
Set up chairs in a circle.

Class Steps
1. Instruct the students to begin walking around the chairs when the music starts. Students walk until the music stops.
2. When the music stops, they should each find a seat.
3. Remove one of the chairs and begin again. When the music stops, two students must share a chair. (Instruct them to be respectful of one another and careful so that the game doesn't become rough. Let students know that the extra person can choose to stand if he or she would rather not share a chair.)
4. Remove another chair and repeat.
5. Continue until only a few chairs remain. Several students will probably be left standing.
6. Finally, explain that you've decided to change the rules of "Musical Chairs" and the point now is for everyone to find a space anywhere in the room—other than on the chairs—to sit down once the music stops.
7. Play one final round.

Follow-up Discussion
1. What did it feel like to play this game at first? How about when we took away more chairs? How about when we changed the rules?
2. Did the chairs seem more valuable at the beginning of the game or at the end?
3. Could you all find places to sit by the end of the game? How about when the rules were changed? Why or why not?
4. How is this game like what happens in a community when critical structures are removed or damaged? What happens to the other components when a crucial one is removed?

LESSON 6

We See the World Through Our Own Lens

One fall day when Chris was young, he was deer hunting in a forest and came upon a small stream in the midst of thick vegetation. The stream was wide enough to prevent him from reaching his destination, which lay on the other side. He followed the stream until he came to a place where a second stream joined the first to form a "Y."

The additional volume of water and dense foliage compounded the challenge of crossing, because Chris now had to cross either two streams above the "Y" or a larger stream below. At length, he noticed a small, mostly hidden delta in the arms of the "Y." Because he was following a deer trail, Chris wondered why the deer hadn't crossed the stream at this juncture. Clearly, a deer could easily have jumped from the trail to the delta, and then onto the trail on the far side. Unfortunately, youthful impatience led Chris to leap the first stream even as he pondered the question.

An answer to his question arrived swiftly. Chris's feet had no sooner touched the solid-looking, sandy surface of the delta than he was up to his chest in quicksand and gooey muck, still holding his hunting rifle, with no sense of where the solid bottom of the ground might be. However, as often happens in life, a difficult circumstance contains the seed of its own solution, if only it can be seen.

In this case, the vegetation that had earlier prevented Chris from crossing the stream now came to his aid. Since both streams were draped in an overhead net of vine maple, he could put the barrel of his rifle across several branches at once, grab the other end, and begin working his way to dry land. After two or three hours of slow, intensive labor, Chris freed himself from the clutching ooze.

Once free, he stripped off his clothes, rinsed them in the stream, and put them back on. They dried as he continued walking along the larger stream until he found a place where the trail led to the other side. And so he learned never to step on a stream's delta that had not been trodden upon by an animal at least as large and heavy as a raccoon, otter, or beaver.

Moreover, from that day to this, the delta reminds Chris that "appearance" is just that—an appearance, which may or may not indicate what lies beneath the surface.

Things Are Not Always What They Seem

We don't see things as they are. We see things as we are.
ANAÏS NIN

Chris formerly studied tiger beetles. One fascinating aspect of the tiger beetle's makeup is that it is devoid of pigment but appears in brilliant metallic hues. Rather than containing pigment, the colors exhibited by tiger beetles are created by light refracted from the sculpted surface of their wing covers and external skeletons.

Chris first noticed this phenomenon when he was examining an Oregon tiger beetle, *Cicindela oregona,* under a binocular scope (powerful binoculars with microscope capabilities). Although the beetle's background color appeared a dull brown, under the microscope every color of the rainbow dazzled the eye.

Like the background color of the Oregon tiger beetle, our world is filled with unseen wonders that are not at first what they appear to be. There is an often-hidden beauty to the biodiversity that surrounds us. When we look closely and change our perspective, we may see that diversity in its myriad dimensions is the hidden wealth of our classroom, school, village, town, city, and nation.

PENNY FOR YOUR THOUGHTS

Purpose

For students to begin to recognize how their own experiences and ways of thinking affect how they see and understand things in the world around them.

Materials

- Five sheets of paper, a penny, and a pencil for each student
- Magnifying glasses (one per small group)

Class Steps

1. Pass out pennies, paper, and pencils to each student. Have students examine the penny, put it away, and then draw what they remember. Put the drawings away.
2. Pass out more paper and have students draw the same penny while they examine it. Put the drawings away.
3. Now give small groups of students a magnifying glass to examine their penny. Tell them to put their penny away and draw it in detail from memory. Put the drawings away.
4. Finally, ask students to draw the penny while examining it with the magnifying glass.
5. When students complete the fourth sketch, tell them to arrange the four drawings side by side, beginning with the first and ending with the most recent.
6. Using a clean piece of paper, ask students to explain the differences between each of their drawings on half of the paper, and to explain the similarities between each of the drawings on the other half of the paper.

Follow-up Discussion

1. How did your drawings change throughout the activity?
2. How did your memory of the penny's design influence the way you drew it?
3. Will this exercise cause you to think differently about things you think you know well?
4. If so, how will you change your thinking?
5. Why is it important to change your thinking as you learn to understand things differently?

TAKING IT TO THE NEXT LEVEL
EVERYTHING WE DO IS AN EXERCISE IN RELATIONSHIPS

Level 1

Encourage your students to think about how their own mind-set affects their interactions with the world. For one day, students should practice being unfriendly by purposely looking away every time they pass someone they don't know. On the second day they should be friendly but quiet, smiling and not saying anything. And on the third day they should smile and say hello, as if everyone they meet is a good friend or potential good friend. Reconvene the group for a discussion of what students experienced and how they felt during the exercise.

Level 2

Ask students to write two poems or short essays. The first can be about any topic they choose. The second poem can be about anything other than the topic of the first poem, but must use at least 10 of the words from the first poem (more if possible). Have students share their poems with the class, and discuss how the meaning and impact of the words change depending on how they are used.

Level 3

Have students investigate a school, community, national, or international issue that interests or concerns them. Begin by having students brainstorm a list of things they care about beyond their own general needs and interests. (See *Resource 3: What Do You Care About?* on page 17.)

Next, ask students to narrow the list to one topic for the whole class to address, or divide the class into groups and have each group plan to address one topic.

At your next meeting, have each person bring to the group one piece of information about the topic: an article, a report, an essay or other opinion piece, photos, or other item. Challenge your students to be creative in their information gathering, and let them know that you will be taking additional action on the issue down the line.

What Do You Care About?

It takes a lot of courage to know who you are and what you want.
ANONYMOUS

☐ **Animals** (rights, rescue, care, protection)

☐ **Education** (policies, curriculum, resources, funding)

☐ **Environment** (water, air, waste, soil)

☐ **Finding or creating safe places for youth to hang out or families to meet**

☐ **Health care** (access, quality, affordability)

☐ **Helping people from different backgrounds or communities work together and get along**

☐ **HIV/AIDS or other disease education or awareness**

☐ **Homelessness**

☐ **Human rights**

☐ **Peace**

Adapted with permission from *Step by Step: A Young Person's Guide to Positive Community Change* by the Mosaic Youth Center Board of Directors with Jennifer Griffin-Wiesner (Search Institute, 2001). From *Teaching Kids to Change the World: Lessons to Inspire Social Responsibility for Grades 6–12* by Jennifer Griffin-Wiesner, M.Ed., and Chris Maser, M.S. This page may be reproduced for educational, noncommercial uses only. Copyright © 2008 by Search Institute; 800-888-7828; www.search-institute.org.

Change is a Universal Constant

The most beautiful thing we can experience is the mystical.
It is the source of all true art and science.
Albert Einstein (1879–1955), German physicist

Change is a continuum that may reach a momentary pinnacle of harmony with our senses. In these moments, we may perceive a fleeting sense of perfection . . . of things being just as we want them to be.

And then, the very change process that creates harmony also takes it away and replaces it with something else—always something else, if only with another condition of itself. For example, one of your students brings you an apple that is not quite ripe, so you place it in your desk with the intention of letting it ripen before you eat it.

What does it mean to ripen? It means the apple continues to change from its original state as you received it (unripe and thus inedible), to another state (ripe and edible), to yet another state (forgotten, it becomes unfit for eating). And change continues even after you discard the apple.

A challenge for all people is that we think in "snapshots"—mental images of conditions we try to hold as constants in our lives. We too often strive for what we determine to be perfection, and then we want, or even expect, that condition to last. Yet nothing in the entire universe can be kept constant—not even snapshots, whether on paper or in our minds. The abiding paradox is that change itself is a constant.

LESSON 7

Sustainability and Change Are Continual Processes

Because change is a constant process, sustainability must also be a continual process of using something and then being the source of its renewal. A good example is growing a vegetable garden, which uses nutrients from the soil, and then replenishing those nutrients with compost. In other words, the soil will feed you as long as you feed the soil.

If, however, you feed the soil only once and then expect its fertility to remain undiminished while you grow crop after crop (taking nutrients out of the soil with each harvest without replacing them), you will be sorely disappointed. In the same way, if you continuously withdraw fixed principal in your savings account in excess of the interest it earns, it's only a matter of time before your savings become depleted because you didn't manage the account for sustainability over the long term.

Because it is often misused, it's appropriate to examine the meaning of the word "resource" (re, meaning "to put back, to restore" and source, "the original supply, the point of something's origin"). Interpreting the word from its roots can be the inspiration for the rebirth of its original meaning—to use something and also to be the source of its renewal.

Our growing realization of the ecological interdependence among all life forms and their physical environments leads us to understand that even seemingly renewable resources show signs of suffering from the effects of society's materialistic demands for more and more, which in turn degrades the renewability of resources in both quality and quantity.

ACTIVITY
EASTER ISLAND

Purpose
Students grasp what happens when a community misunderstands resource to mean something that can be consumed indefinitely without renewal and reinvestment.

Materials
- Copies of *Resource 4: The Rise and Fall of Easter Island* on page 21

Preparation
Read the story in advance before sharing it with your class.

Class Steps
1. Read *Resource 4: The Rise and Fall of Easter Island.* The story describes the natural history of Easter Island, an isolated South Pacific island 2,400 miles off the coast of Chile.
2. Does the story of Easter Island reflect what is happening today worldwide? Offer similar examples in your own community of creatures that are endangered or extinct, or of demands for scarce open land or quality housing, or local shortages of food, electricity, or other resources, and so on.
3. Ask your students to speak with a parent or other elder about one of the examples you identify to find out how things were similar or different in past years (e.g., perhaps the elder was alive when a certain animal still lived in your area).

The Rise and Fall of Easter Island

Easter Island is a tiny, 43-square-mile piece of land in the South Pacific, 2,400 miles off the western coast of South America. The island's oldest pollen dates (analyses of pollen from certain ancient plants) go back some 30,000 years, long before the island's first people arrived. At that time, based on the pollen record, the island was forested with now-extinct, giant Jubaea palms.

Polynesians settled on the island around 1200 A.D. They began gradually to clear the land for agriculture and cut trees to build canoes. The island, though small, was relatively fertile, the sea teemed with fish, and the people flourished. The population rose to about 3,000 or 4,000, and probably remained relatively stable. Eventually, trees were cut to provide logs for transportation and to erect hundreds of stone statues, or moai, some of which are roughly 32 feet high and weigh as much as 85 tons.

Deforestation, which began shortly after the first people arrived, was almost complete 500 years later by 1700. The pollen record reflects that when trees were cut, they did not grow back. When the Europeans discovered Easter Island in 1722, it was treeless and in a state of decline. Nevertheless, Dutch explorer Jacob Roggeveen and the commanders of his three ships described the island as "exceedingly fruitful, producing bananas, potatoes, sugar-cane of remarkable thickness, and many other kinds of fruits of the earth." If the soil was rich enough for these plants, then why did the trees not grow back?

As it turns out, the Polynesians brought rats with them in their boats. As the human population expanded, the people were busy cutting down trees. Meanwhile, the rat population also expanded, and the rats ate more and more of the palm nuts, which prevented new tree growth. The effects of drought, wind, and soil erosion could also have accelerated the island's deforestation. In addition, both people and rats exploited many of the island's other resources, such as its abundance of birds' eggs. The downward spiral had begun.

Deforestation meant there were no trees available to build canoes for fishing. Soil erosion led to reduced crop yields. And the eggs of the sooty tern were probably exploited to the point that the bird no longer nested on the island.

Fewer fish, eggs, and crops inevitably led to a shortage of food. Hunger, in turn, eventually brought the civilization to the brink of collapse. Today, all that remains of the original culture of Easter Island are the coastal statues that once stood upright on specially built platforms. Others lie abandoned between the volcanic quarries of their origin and their planned destinations, and still others remain unfinished in the quarries.[1]

From *Teaching Kids to Change the World: Lessons to Inspire Social Responsibility for Grades 6–12* by Jennifer Griffin-Wiesner, M.Ed., and Chris Maser, M.S. This page may be reproduced for educational, noncommercial uses only. Copyright © 2008 by Search Institute; 800-888-7828; www.search-institute.org.

Cumulative Effects, Lag Periods, and Thresholds Are Key

To understand the basic elements of a physical system, consider snowflakes. When snowflakes begin falling, they first land on warm soil and melt, entering the ground without a trace. One after another, they come into view, fall past us, and land, only to disappear seemingly as rapidly as they appeared.

In reality, each snowflake does something as it touches the soil: its coolness dissipates the soil's heat. As snowflake after snowflake touches the ground and melts, there is a cumulative effect: the ground is eventually cooled enough that falling snowflakes melt progressively more slowly, until some don't melt at all. Now snow begins to gradually accumulate until the ground is covered in a blanket of white.

How many snowflakes have to melt before the ground is cool enough for those yet falling to be noticed? Each snowflake's coolness is part of the cumulative effect, and the time it takes to notice the first visibly remaining snowflake on the soil is the lag period. Once the soil is cold enough for the first snowflake to visibly remain on the soil surface, the threshold in soil temperature—and your conscious awareness—has been crossed.

Is one snowflake more important than another? Is the one you see sparkling in the sun more important than the one that melted upon landing? Although your relationships with each of them differ, neither is more or less important than another. Without those that have melted and cooled the soil, the snowflakes that ultimately form the blanket of white would not have survived to do so. Now, let's consider the reverse.

As the air temperature warms, snow begins to melt, one flake at a time. Do you see the cumulative effect of the first, second, and third snowflake melting? How long must snowflakes melt (the lag period) before the threshold is crossed and you notice the effect of the melting?

An example of cumulative effects, lag periods, and thresholds in a living system can be seen in the evolution of an apple. It evolves from a pollinated flower to a small, unripe fruit, to a ripe fruit, to an overripe fruit, to a rotten fruit, to a seed, to a tree, to a pollinated flower, to an unripe fruit, in a never-ending cycle.

One day, your student picks an apple while it's still green and brings it to you. Since it's not yet ripe, you store it in your desk drawer and later forget it's there. Nevertheless, the chemical process of ripening—changes in weight, color, texture, and so on—continues. These minute changes represent the cumulative effects embodied in processes of continual change. The time it takes for these minute changes to become readily noticeable is the lag period, which you might not notice unless you pay particular attention on a daily basis to certain measurable changes signifying a threshold of visibility. In the case of the apple, the cumulative effects of ripening take the apple past the threshold of edibility to soft, mushy inedibility.

ACTIVITY
AN APPLE A DAY

Purpose
For students to learn how the concepts of cumulative effects, lag period, and threshold come into play when they are involved in efforts to change something for the better.

Materials
- A piece of unripe fruit (such as an apple, pear, or banana)
- A camera
- *Resource 5: Daily Observation Record* and *Resource 6: Three-Day Interval Observation Record* (page 24)

Class Steps

1. Place the unripe fruit where everyone can observe it. Beginning on Day One, photograph the fruit, and do so each day until you discard it. Do not review the photos.

2. Record in a daily log the changes you see taking place (don't mention your observations to your students).

3. Ask half the class to record the changes they see in the fruit on a daily basis, using *Resource 5: Daily Interval Observation Record.*

4. Ask the other half of the class to record the changes they see every third day, using *Resource 6: Three-Day Interval Observation Record.*

5. Ask both groups of students (and include yourself) to note the day on which the fruit is considered ripe enough to eat, when its ripeness is perfect, and the day when it passes beyond the edible stage.

6. Continue the observations until the fruit is so rotten it must be discarded. Do not allow either group to see the other's work. (That goes for you and your notes as well!)

7. After discarding the fruit, align the photographs in sequence and have the students help you determine on which day the different changes become evident. Those noticeable changes represent *thresholds*.

8. Next, get out all three sets of written observations and see how well they correspond to the photographic evidence.

9. Which observations come closest to matching the visible evidence of the photos? Why?

10. Once you have all agreed upon and recorded the threshold events, repeat the experiment with a new piece of fruit, paying particular attention to minute changes leading up to a threshold and using the photographs as a reference.

11. When you're trying to make changes in the world around you, how can you notice and keep track of the difference you're making? How can you know whether your actions are having an impact?

LESSON 9

All Change Is to Some Extent Irreversible

What happens when water freezes in a pipe? For some, the mere mention of frozen pipes sends chills up and down the spine.

Under normal circumstances, water exists in liquid form as it flows through a pipe. But as air temperature drops, water in an uninsulated pipe slowly freezes. As water molecules expand near their freezing point, so much pressure is exerted on the pipe's interior that it can burst, which often goes unnoticed until the weather warms up and ice melts once again into a liquid—a situation that happens to some folks every winter.

When a pipe ruptures, it is forever altered, while the water within it returns to its liquid state. Thus, one part of the event seems reversible—the physical state of the water can move from liquid to frozen to liquid again. The pipe rupture, on the other hand, is irreversible, which means that as long as water runs through it, leaking will occur from the damaged section, which must be replaced before the plumbing system as a whole can once again function properly.

Another example of irreversible damage might be what occurs when a dairy farmer drains a wetland area to make pasture land for her milk cows. She digs a series of ditches to lead water away from the swamp, and effectively lowers the level of the water table. In so doing, the farmer changes the wetland into a pasture, unwittingly eliminating a rare orchid

Daily Observation Record

Name _____   Type of fruit _____

DAY	DESCRIPTION	CHANGES SINCE LAST OBSERVATION
1		
2		
3		
4		
5		
6		
7		
8		
9		
10		

From *Teaching Kids to Change the World: Lessons to Inspire Social Responsibility for Grades 6–12* by Jennifer Griffin-Wiesner, M.Ed., and Chris Maser, M.S. This page may be reproduced for educational, noncommercial uses only. Copyright © 2008 by Search Institute; 800-888-7828; www.search-institute.org.

Three-Day Interval Observation Record

Name _____   Type of fruit _____

DAY	DESCRIPTION	CHANGES SINCE LAST OBSERVATION
1		
4		
7		
10		

From *Teaching Kids to Change the World: Lessons to Inspire Social Responsibility for Grades 6–12* by Jennifer Griffin-Wiesner, M.Ed., and Chris Maser, M.S. This page may be reproduced for educational, noncommercial uses only. Copyright © 2008 by Search Institute; 800-888-7828; www.search-institute.org.

habitat, despite the fact that the pasture remains a pasture only as long as the drainage ditches are functional.

The orchid is then added to the endangered species list and the dairy farmer is ordered to reclaim the swamp, so she refills the ditches. Although the water table rises in the short term and the land once again becomes swampy, it takes much longer for swamp life to return. Although the swamp habitat is recreated, the orchid does not return, and thus the functional interactions of the swamp are never quite the same as they would have been had the swamp not been drained in the first place.

ACTIVITY
BIT O' HONEY

Purpose
For students to observe the changes in the honey, realizing that even when they re-create the original conditions, the changes that have occurred have had lasting impact.

Materials
- Three jars
- A variety of honey that crystallizes relatively quickly, such as clover honey*
- Plastic spoons or wooden sticks for sampling
- Sheet of paper and pencil for each student
- Calendar
- Liquid thermometer
- Sauce pan
- Water source

* *Note:* The honey usually found in supermarkets can take months to crystallize, although cooling it can speed up the process.

Preparation
Pour honey into each jar.

Class Steps
1. Give students a small honey sample to taste.
2. Ask students to describe on paper how they would characterize the honey sample—flavor, texture, consistency, etc.
3. Place the three jars of honey where everyone can see them, and put a calendar next to each jar. Honey turns into sugar crystals when left at room temperature over time (the amount of glucose in the honey determines how quickly it crystallizes).
4. Record the class's daily observations of the honey samples on the calendar.
5. Discuss:
   - Do you see anything happening on a daily basis?
   - When did you notice the first change? Describe it.
   - When is the process of crystallization complete? How can you tell?
6. Discuss:
   - What happens when you place one jar of crystallized honey in a pot of lukewarm water?
   - What happens when you place the second jar of honey in a sauce pan of hot tap water (at no more than 100°F)?
   - What happens when you place the third jar of the honey in a pan of very hot tap water (at no more than 120°F)?
   - How close does the honey in each jar come to its original state? How long does it take?
   - How would you define "original state"?
   - Will the honey change states when it cools?
   - Has the process of crystallization been completely reversed, based on the original descriptions of the honey before its crystallization?
7. What do these two exercises tell us about change? Is change reversible?

LESSON 10

We Live in the Invisible Present

We live in what can be described as the invisible present. We do not perceive slow, subtle changes, such as the daily growth of a child or the quiet opening of a flower; nor do we often perceive more dramatic changes, such as the gradual disappearance of old things in the wake of advancing technology or long-term changes in climate.

Parents and caregivers often take a series of dated snapshots of a child's physical growth or measure the child's advancing height against the side of a doorframe. Of course, relatives who visit only once or twice a year are more likely to immediately notice the height and growth changes in the child. Similarly, the opening of a flower can be witnessed through time-lapse photography, but not ordinarily by sitting in a chair keeping constant watch over the blossom.

To grasp long-term changes, such as in the earth's climate, requires our memory and constant monitoring. The present moment, the "here and now," is all we have. If we focus elsewhere, we miss forever our chance to participate fully in the present life.

ACTIVITY

NO TIME LIKE THE PRESENT

Purpose

For students to observe the incremental changes that occur over time.

Materials

- Digital camera
- Computer or other means for viewing digital photos

Preparation

Noah Kalina ("Noah K."), a professional photographer from Brooklyn, New York, has taken daily photos of himself since 2000 and posted them on his Web site at everyday.noahkalina. com. Review Noah K.'s digital photographs and then help your students start a similar photographic project documenting incremental changes in your classroom or school building, a street corner or particular tree, or another subject.

Class Steps

1. Choose a subject or a series of subjects, the frequency with which you will photograph them, and the length of time over which you will photograph them.
2. Remind your students to be consistent in taking their photos.
3. When the time period has passed, lay out the photos in chronological order.

Follow-up Discussion

Talk about the changes you observe in the photographs: What stays the same? What changes do you notice?

TAKING IT TO THE NEXT LEVEL

CHANGE IS A UNIVERSAL CONSTANT

Level 1

Your students may not believe they have much power in the world, especially if they've tried, unsuccessfully, to make their voices heard in the past. Use these simple activities from *Shoulder to Shoulder: Stories and Strategies of Youth-Adult Partnerships That Succeed* by Deborah Fisher (Search Institute, 2004) to empower young people to overcome age bias.

- Role-play situations in which young people stand up for themselves in order to be heard. "It's important to give youth the skills, words, and role playing—to tell them to not let adults treat them disrespectfully," says Darby Neptune of Handz On.

- Help youth identify and talk about things adults do that alienate or shut them down (ignoring their comments, talking about them as if they weren't present, or telling them they won't be able to understand something without the opportunity to try).

- Let young people know they have the right to peacefully and respectfully confront adults who do these things.

Level 2

Ask your students to write a story or create a visual work of art that represents living in the present: that now—right now, this very minute—is all the time we really ever have, and if we miss it, we've lost it forever.

Level 3

Using the brainstormed list of things they care about (see page 16), help your students investigate proposed changes in local or state policies or plans regarding these topics. It will be easier to research the issues when Congress (or your State House and Senate) is in session or elections are forthcoming, but you can also contact your local or state representatives for more information.

Be persistent and teach your students that their elected leaders are in place to serve them. The following Web site can be a good starting point for your fact gathering: www.usa.gov.

Act Locally and Affect the Whole World

"Why, sometimes I've believed as many as six impossible things before breakfast."

The White Queen in *Alice in Wonderland* by Lewis Carroll

The first ditch might have been an idle scratch in the surface of the ground made by a child playing in a rain puddle. The child, with no grand scheme in mind, dug the little trench that allowed water to flow from where it was to where it would not otherwise have gone—a simple, innocent act with no particular outcome anticipated. Once the outcome became clear, though, the child's next little ditch had a purpose—to see if water would behave the same way a second time, and then a third, and to see how far water would follow a ditch, and so on.

Somewhere in time, a man or a woman had a budding idea, and then the conscious thought of leading water from one place to another for a specific purpose—a purpose beyond play and mere curiosity. That one thought, that one experiment in the control of water for a specific, practical end, forever changed the world and humanity's relationship to it. The first ditch dug purposefully turned water into a commodity that could be moved from place to place, owned, stored, bought and sold, stolen, and fought over.

Because of ditches, humanity, plants, and animals were able to live in previously uninhabited places because water could now be had in close proximity to the life that depended on it. Ditches helped give rise to agriculture and eventually led to such feats of engineering as the Suez and Panama Canals, each of which physically connects one ocean with another. The first ditch irrevocably altered humanity's view of itself, its sense of society, and its ability to manipulate nature.

LESSON 11

Our Actions Have Consequences

Can we control the consequences of our actions in the world?

We introduce thoughts, practices, substances, and technologies into our communities and the wider world, and we usually think of those introductions in terms of development. Whatever we introduce in the name of development will determine how the world will respond to our presence and our cultural necessities. Therefore, it's to our social benefit to pay close attention to what we introduce.

As a case in point, before urban sprawl began to consume the North American desert, the area around Phoenix, Arizona, was a haven for people who suffered from allergies. In the 1940s and 1950s, doctors sent patients there because the dry air was virtually pollen-free. However, as is the case with most, if not all, human migrations, people also brought favorite things with them from home, including nonnative plants. Those plants matured and now fill the desert air with pollen each spring. In addition, the dry desert climate causes pollen grains from nonnative plants to remain aloft and ride the air currents, wafting on every zephyr. They are not washed from dry desert air as they are in nondesert areas that experience spring rains.

And so the very people who moved to Phoenix to find relief from allergens unwittingly positioned Arizona among the top 10 percent of U.S. states in pollen count during the six-week allergy season. Allergy sufferers themselves inadvertently turned their desert haven into their worst nightmare because they did not identify and protect the environmental value they were drawn to in the first place—air virtually free of pollen.[2]

While the actions we take always represent both our sense of values and our personal behavior, they also initiate a never-ending story of cause and effect, often to our detriment. Our values, to which we many times give no conscious thought, shape the contours of our lives. This is largely because we don't always attempt to calculate the risk of an event that has never before occurred and which may seem unlikely to occur in the future, such as the introduction of nonnative plants into the Phoenix ecology, where airborne pollen has become a permanent feature of the desert air.

ACTIVITY
DYE-ING FOR WATER

Purpose
To demonstrate the difficulty of preventing new elements from altering an environment.

Materials
- Three or more porous flowers (such as daisies, daffodils, or Queen Anne's lace, which readily absorb dye from water into the veins of their petals)
- Containers for the flowers
- Water
- Food coloring

Preparation
Place each flower in a separate container of water.

Class Steps
1. Keep one flower as a control (don't add dye to its water). Put dye into the water of the second container and observe what happens.
2. Give the third flower to students. Have them add dye to the third container of water. Ask students to see if they can devise a way to prevent dye in the water from being absorbed by the flower—dye that they must leave in the water. (You can also bring several flowers and have students work in small groups.)

Follow-up Discussion

1. Could you prevent the dye from being absorbed by the flower once the dye was added to the water? How much control did you have over the dye absorption?
2. What techniques did you try?
3. What can you learn from this exercise about what happens when we introduce new elements into our environment?
4. The intended goal is to give the flower the water it needs. Dye represents an unintended, negative consequence that is unwittingly added to an environment. How can we anticipate and avoid negative consequences?

LESSON 12

Consider the Long-Term Consequences *First*

A group protesting relentless political pressure by the representatives of an absentee energy company owner once retained Chris as an expert witness. The company and its supporters were determined to situate an electricity-generating plant in the midst of an established neighborhood. The potential long-term results? Pollution not only of the air, but also of Laughing Creek, a waterway that emptied into a nearby river and from there into a lake (which was the municipal water supply for a large city), and ultimately into the Gulf of Mexico.

Company officials and lawyers acted with a single objective—to build the energy plant, despite opposition from local residents and in the face of likely social and environmental consequences. Chris was engaged as a systems thinker to ask relevant questions of company officials that citizens themselves did not know how to ask. His objective was to represent the interests of present and future residents who would be affected by the plant's operation in hidden, and progressively more negative, environmental ways.

When a major social or environmental change is at hand, it is important to assess risks and potential consequences. One way to become informed is to read environmental impact statements (EIS), which are assessments of potential consequences of federal environmental actions. Search for EIS papers at nucat.library.northwestern.edu.

ACTIVITY
A COLORFUL TURN OF EVENTS

Purpose
To demonstrate the importance of asking questions before introducing long-term change and its consequences.

Materials
- Four medium-size glass jars
- Water
- Sand
- Soil
- Shredded paper
- A small potted plant with white or light-colored flowers (daisies or daffodils)
- Three bottles of food coloring
- An eyedropper
- Pencils and copies of *Resource 7: Decisions, Decisions* on page 33

Preparation
Fill one jar with water, one with sand, one with soil, and one with shredded paper.

Class Steps—Part 1
1. Divide the class into two groups and label them "adults" and "children."
2. Explain that the "adults" are to change the environment in each of the jars by squeezing a full dropper of food coloring into each of the four jars without consulting the "children."

Follow-up Discussion—Part 1
Ask the "children" to discuss the following questions:

1. What happens when food coloring touches the water, sand, soil, or shredded paper?
2. Can you remove the food coloring from any of the jars without disturbing the water, sand, soil, or shredded paper?
3. Can you remove the food coloring from any of the jars by removing whatever is dyed by the coloring?
4. How do you know whether you removed all the food coloring?
5. Is there any jar from which you cannot remove the food coloring?
6. What would happen if the "adults" were to squeeze more and more food coloring into each of the jars? Would you, or they, be able to control what the coloring does or where it goes?

Class Step—Part 2

Have the "adults" water the plant with colored water for one week.

Follow-up Discussion—Part 2

Ask the entire class to discuss the following questions:

1. Can you control what happens once the food coloring enters the plant's vascular system? If not, why not?
2. What have you learned about the amount of control humans have when a toxic substance is introduced into the environment? If it seeps through the soil into a ditch, and is washed into a stream, a river, and on to the ocean, does it have anywhere else to go?
3. Now that you've seen what happens to water and plants in the jars, what questions would you ask if chemicals were going to be flushed into the river or reservoir from which your drinking water comes?
4. What questions would you ask if chemicals were going to be buried in the soil, where groundwater could wash them into the well from which you got your drinking water? Why is it important to ask these questions?
5. Pass out copies of *Resource 7: Decisions, Decisions*. Have students answer each question and share their answers with the group.

LESSON 13
There's Always a Trade-off

Our thoughts and actions have consequences, both seen and unforeseen. For example, in the mid-1950s, the U.S. Army Corps of Engineers built a dam across the Columbia River, which forms the border between Washington and Oregon. The dam was designed to produce electricity and store water for crop irrigation (a positive benefit for farmers).

Unexpectedly, when water filled the pool behind the completed dam, the high water level inundated and effectively destroyed the habitat of the already-threatened Columbian white-tailed deer (a negative consequence for the deer). In the late 1960s, the Columbian white-tailed deer were declared an endangered species. The Corps of Engineers was ordered to mitigate the situation by creating a suitable habitat for the deer to replace what was lost. However, in the process of artificially creating a new habitat for the Columbian white-tailed deer (a positive consequence for the deer), more than 300 other plant and animal species lost their habitat (a negative consequence for all).

ACTIVITY
THERE'S NO GOING BACK

Purpose
Young people understand that once something is altered, it is forever changed, regardless of any additional steps that may be taken.

Decisions, Decisions

Individually, or with a partner or small group, answer the following questions:

1. What things do you see adults doing in your community (or in the wider world) without first consulting young people?

_____

_____

_____

_____

_____

2. How might you make decisions differently?

_____

_____

_____

_____

3. What are effective ways that you and other young people can make your opinions heard?

_____

_____

_____

_____

4. How can you change the way some decisions are made?

_____

_____

_____

_____

From *Teaching Kids to Change the World: Lessons to Inspire Social Responsibility for Grades 6–12* by Jennifer Griffin-Wiesner, M.Ed., and Chris Maser, M.S. This page may be reproduced for educational, noncommercial uses only. Copyright © 2008 by Search Institute; 800-888-7828; www.search-institute.org

Materials

- One 3- or 4-foot piece of 2 x 4 wood
- Four or six 12-inch pieces of lath (thin wood strips from a building supply store)
- Several small finishing nails
- One or two small hammers
- Squeeze tube of wood glue
- Magnifying glass
- Copies of *Resource 8: Egypt's Aswan High Dam—Gains and Losses*

Preparation

Read *Resource 8: Egypt's Aswan High Dam—Gains and Losses* as background preparation.

Class Steps

1. Have two students each nail a separate piece of lath to the 2 x 4 (just deep enough that the nail and lath can be pulled off the 2 x 4 with relative ease).
2. Ask:
   - What remains when the lath and its nail are removed from the 2 x 4?
   - Pull the nail out of the lath: what do you see?
   - Using the magnifying glass, do you see any marks on the nail you used that are not visible on an unused nail?
   - Is there a way to attach the lath to the 2 x 4 without leaving a mark on the lath, 2 x 4, or nail?
3. Have students use wood glue to accomplish the same objective.
4. Ask:
   - When the glue is dry, can you separate the lath from the 2 x 4 without leaving any evidence of glue on either the 2 x 4 or the lath?
   - How much glue do you have left over to use on another project? Do you have as much glue now as you once had?
   - Has the shape of the glue tube re- the same or become deformed?
   - Can you reshape the glue tube and put glue back into it so that you can use it

again for something else? If not, why can't you restore the tube of glue to its former shape and contents?

Follow-up Discussion

1. What are the trade-offs of your actions in this situation?
2. What happens if you start to alter something and then change your mind? Can you put things back the way they were?
3. Can you think of something—anything— you do that does not produce a trade-off of some kind?
4. Read through *Resource 8: Egypt's Aswan High Dam—Gains and Losses* with students and discuss lessons learned.

TAKING IT TO THE NEXT LEVEL
ACT LOCALLY AND AFFECT THE WHOLE WORLD

Level 1

Visit your local water-treatment plant to learn about the substances that homes and businesses discharge into the water supply. How are chemicals, waste products, and bacteria treated? What effects might untreated water have on animal and plant life in local rivers? What kinds of effects might untreated water have on ocean life when combined with sewage discharge from other cities? How many people around the world draw their sustenance from the ocean? What is a community's responsibility to other people when it comes to caring for water, a necessity for all life?

Level 2

Have students reread *Resource 8: Egypt's Aswan High Dam—Gains and Losses*. Have them research the environmental costs of building other dams, such as China's Three Gorges dam or the Tennessee Valley Authority dams. Ask students to choose one dam and prepare posters presenting the pro and cons of the project. Who and what did the dam help? Who and what were harmed? Do the dam's benefits outweigh its drawbacks? Provide a variety of viewpoints.

Level 3

Ask students to research a controversial issue facing the legislature, city council, or other political body, and prepare a list of questions about its local and global implications. Make arrangements to visit with community leaders to learn their views, the actions they support, and how they envision the community changing over time as a result. Have your students write letters in response and send them to the officials they met and/or to the editor of your local newspaper. Help youth brainstorm ways to follow up if they do not receive a response.

Egypt's Aswan High Dam— Gains and Losses

While working as a vertebrate zoologist north of the Sudanese border along the Nile River in Egypt in 1963 and 1964, Chris and his scientific expedition team members met with an official of the Egyptian Ministry of Agriculture. The government's focus was on harnessing waterpower to generate electricity and provide crop irrigation. The scientists were concerned that a new dam across the Nile River would damage the surrounding ecology.

Chris and his colleagues explained that building the dam would increase the geographic distribution of snails carrying parasitic worms, which would ultimately lead to widespread and debilitating human infection with Schistosomiasis. At the time, water above the present Aswan Dam was still snail-free and safe to swim in, because the water was too swift and cold for the snails' survival. Water below the dam was a different matter: it was already unsafe to swim in or catch frogs in those waters, because the snails were already present.

Further, constructing the Aswan High Dam would cause the Nile River to fill with silt, starving the Nile Delta farmland downriver of its annual supply of nutrient-rich sediment, as well as degrading the Mediterranean end of the Nile Delta. Chris and his colleagues explained that the dam could also become a military target, just as German dams had become British targets during World War II.

The engineers building the Aswan High Dam had intended only to store more water and produce electricity, which they ultimately did. However, when the dam was completed in 1970, it also began intercepting the nutrient-rich sediments destined for the Mediterranean Sea. Without the silt of the Nile's

annual floodwaters, which nourished organisms at the base of the food chain in estuaries and near-shore water, the population of sardines off the coast of the Nile Delta diminished by 97% within two years. In addition, the rich delta, which had been growing in size for thousands of years, became (and continues to be) eroded by the Mediterranean, because the Nile no longer deposits silt at its mouth.[3]

Until the Aswan High Dam was built, the annual sediment-laden waters of the Nile added a millimeter of nutrient-rich silt to farms along the river each year. Now that flooding has been stopped by the new dam, silt not only collects upriver from the dam (where it diminishes the dam's holding capacity), but also is no longer being deposited on riverside farms, thus decreasing their fertility.

The time will come when the farmers will have to buy commercial fertilizer, a burden most farmers can probably not afford. In addition, because irrigation without flooding causes the soil to become saline, the Nile Valley, which has been farmed continuously for 5,000 years, may have to be abandoned within a few centuries.

In the meantime, schistosomiasis has indeed spread southward to the Sudan, raising the question: Does one nation have the right to knowingly cause the spread of a highly infectious disease to another nation in the name of economic self-interest, or for any other reason, without the recipient nation's permission?

One unexpected consequence of building the Aswan High Dam relates to the local rat population. The Nile annually flooded many nooks, crannies, and caves along its edge, killing rats whose fleas carry bubonic plague. Because floods along the Nile no longer occur, the rat population has soared, and bubonic plague is once again a potential public health threat.

From *Teaching Kids to Change the World: Lessons to Inspire Social Responsibility for Grades 6–12* by Jennifer Griffin-Wiesner, M.Ed., and Chris Maser, M.S. This page may be reproduced for educational, noncommercial uses only. Copyright © 2008 by Search Institute; 800-888-7828; www.search-institute.org

Ecology and Economy Are Each One Half of the House We Live In

This we know . . . the earth does not belong to man, man belongs to earth. All things are connected, like the blood which connects one family. Whatever befalls the earth befalls the children of the earth. Man did not weave the web of life—he is merely a strand in it. Whatever he does to the web, he does to himself.

Chief Seattle (1786–1866), Native American tribal leader

"Ecology" and "economy" both come from the Latin root *oeco* and the Greek root *oiko*, meaning "house" (and *oikonomia*, meaning "household management"). Ecology refers to our understanding of the house (its foundation, condition, and biophysical processes), while economy refers to the management and maintenance of the house—and it's the same house.

The availability of choices dictates the amount of control we feel we have, which gives us a sense of security. If the present generation steals from all future generations by exploiting a resource, for example, young people inherit far fewer choices and, thus, a progressively more insecure future.

LESSON 14

Reinvest in Systems As If They're Big Business

In a business model, we earn money (economic capital) and then reinvest a percentage of those earnings (a cost) into such things as equipment and building maintenance. And we do this in order to continue making a profit by protecting the integrity of our initial investment over time. In business, we reinvest economic capital after the fact, after we have earned the profits.

However, when it comes to social and environmental change, we must invest in social and environmental capital before the fact, before the profits are earned. Withdrawals, without the balance of deposits, can only draw down principal over time and thus continue to harm the long-term sustainability of a given system.

Not surprisingly, however, there is disagreement on this approach. When the notion of sustainability arises in a conflict over resources, opposing parties tend to regard opinions and knowledge favorable to their respective sides as "good" data, and discount all unfavorable data as "bad" or "inconclusive" thinking. In this way, a conflict becomes politicized. And when two groups become mired in opposition, it is often impossible for them to see compromise as a shared investment in the future. Unfortunately, this lack of vision continually impoverishes future generations.

ACTIVITY

KEEPING INPUT AND OUTPUT IN BALANCE

Purpose

Young people experience the importance and the challenge of keeping the input and output of resources in balance.

Materials

- Copies of *Resources 9* and *10: Investment and Return* for each student

Class Steps

1. Explain that you are going to plan a hypothetical fund-raiser for your local food shelf. Your goal is to raise $500.
2. Ask the class to brainstorm a list of fund-raising possibilities, such as a car wash, plant sale, or special event like a bike-a-thon, read-a-thon, or walk-a-thon.
3. Using *Resources 9* and *10* on pages 41–42, help students determine the cost of the fund-raising option they choose to pursue ("Estimated Expenses"). You may also want to calculate the cost of advertising, the number of customers you'll need to reach your goal, and any other factors that are relevant to students. (We've used the example of a plant sale in *Resource 9* to show you what we mean.)

4. Have the class determine how they can reach their fund-raising goal using the "Estimated Income" and "Estimated Income Less Expenses" portion of *Resource 10: Investment and Return.*

Follow-up Discussion

1. What did you learn during this process? (If students don't mention it, stress that in order to have a positive outcome—in this case, enough money to donate—they need to invest money up front and then figure out how to keep more dollars coming in than going out.)
2. What else could you do to reach the goal if the first fund-raiser falls short?

LESSON 15

Our "House" Is a Global Commons

The actions we take at home affect the larger world in ways we cannot begin to fathom. And the reverse is true as well: what happens around the globe ought to matter to us, because, while we may feel far away, we are not immune to its effects.

For example, in 1883, a small Indonesian island in the Indian Ocean called Krakatoa, was virtually obliterated by enormous volcanic eruptions that sent ash high enough above the earth to ride the world's air currents for more than a year. This event reduced the amount of sunlight that reached the earth, which in turn cooled the surrounding climate and affected all life.

Just as it carried the volcanic ash of Krakatoa, air also carries the reproductive spores of fungi and the pollen of various trees and grasses, as well as dust and microscopic organisms. In fact, if not for these air currents that circle the earth, the Amazon forest would starve to death.

The wind-scoured, nearly barren southern Sahara Desert of North Africa feeds the

Example of Investment and Return

Example: Plant Sale—Estimated Expenses

ITEM	ESTIMATED EXPENSES
250 perennial garden plants	$2/plant x 250 plants = $500.00 (purchased from local nursery)
Two school custodians for four hours at $20/hour each (to provide school access and support on a weekend morning)	2 custodians x 4 hours x $20/hour = $160.00
Snacks and beverages for 45 volunteers	(45 snacks x $1/snack) + (45 drinks x $1/drink) = $90.00
Total Expenses	**$750.00**

Plant Sale—Estimated Income

ITEM	ESTIMATED INCOME
250 perennial garden plants ($5 per plant)	$5/plant x 250 plants = $1,250.00
Total Income	**$1,250.00**

Plant Sale—Estimated Income Less Expenses

ITEM	ESTIMATED INCOME MINUS EXPENSES
250 perennial garden plants	+ $1,250.00
Plants, custodial salaries, and snacks for volunteers	- $750.00
Total Profit for Food Shelf Donation	**$500.00**

From *Teaching Kids to Change the World: Lessons to Inspire Social Responsibility for Grades 6–12* by Jennifer Griffin-Wiesner, M.Ed., and Chris Maser, M.S. This page may be reproduced for educational, noncommercial uses only. Copyright © 2008 by Search Institute; 800-888-7828; www.search-institute.org.

Investment and Return

Estimated Expenses

ITEM	ESTIMATED EXPENSES

Total Expenses

Estimated Income

ITEM	ESTIMATED INCOME

Total Income

Estimated Income Less Expenses

ITEM	ESTIMATED INCOME MINUS EXPENSES

Total Profit for Donation

From *Teaching Kids to Change the World: Lessons to Inspire Social Responsibility for Grades 6–12* by Jennifer Griffin-Wiesner, M.Ed., and Chris Maser, M.S. This page may be reproduced for educational, noncommercial uses only. Copyright © 2008 by Search Institute; 800-888-7828; www.search-institute.org.

Amazonian forests of South America with mineral-coated dust from the Bodélé depression, which is the largest source of dust in the world. During the northern hemisphere winter, winds routinely blow across this part of North Africa, where they pick up 700,000 tons of dust on an average day and sweep much of it across the Atlantic. Approximately 20 million tons of this mineral-rich dust fall on the Amazon rain forest and enrich its otherwise nutrient-poor soils. The Bodélé depression accounts for only 0.2 percent of the entire Saharan Desert and is only .05 percent of the size of the Amazon itself.[4] However, while air currents carry life-giving oxygen, water, and life-sustaining dust, they also transport toxic pollution—a human legacy.

Air—everyone's birthright—can be likened to the key in this Chinese proverb: "To every man is given the key to the gates of heaven, and the same key opens the gates of hell." Air carries both life-giving oxygen and life-threatening pollution. Fortunately, although air quality decreases as pollution levels increase, rain and snow scrub many pollutants from the air and deposit them into the soil, where they move through the soil along the flow of groundwater.

ACTIVITY
YOU'RE BREATHING WHAT?!

Purpose
For students to see evidence that we are part of an interdependent global commons and that our actions have far-reaching consequences.

Materials
- Petroleum jelly (such as Vaseline)
- String
- Black permanent marker
- 1/2 gallon cardboard milk or juice carton
- Hole punch
- Magnifying glass
- Copies of *Resource 11: Air Quality Experiment Data Sheet*

Class Steps
1. Clean and dry the cardboard carton.
2. Cut the carton along the side folds to make four equal rectangles. Then cut each rectangle into three 3" x 3" squares for a total of 12 squares.
3. On the plain side of each square, draw a 1" x 1" solid black square in the center to provide a contrast for particles that are trapped in the gel.
4. Punch a hole in a corner of each square, and tie a string through the hole. Make sure the string is long enough to hang the square from a tree branch.
5. Choose four different locations at which to measure air quality (on school grounds, at a nearby park, along the edge of a parking lot, inside the school, and so on).
6. Designate three squares per location, and write the name of the location on each square, as well as on *Resource 11: Air Quality Experiment Data Sheet* (page 44).
7. In each location, hang the squares from a convenient site that is unlikely to be disturbed. Add petroleum jelly to each square.
8. Wait three to five days for results. If rain is predicted, it is best to wait until you are likely to have a dry spell.
9. Go back to each location and collect the squares.
10. On-site, if possible, count the number of visible particles in the petroleum jelly. Also write down any other descriptive factors (such as color or texture of the pollutants).
11. Carefully collect the samples. Back in the classroom, compare samples from each site.

Follow-up Discussion
1. How many and what particles did you notice on each square?
2. How do the samples compare from

Air Quality Experiment Data Sheet

LOCATION 1

	SQUARE 1	SQUARE 2	SQUARE 3
Color			
Texture			
Particle Type			
Description			

LOCATION 2

	SQUARE 4	SQUARE 5	SQUARE 6
Color			
Texture			
Particle Type			
Description			

LOCATION 3

	SQUARE 7	SQUARE 8	SQUARE 9
Color			
Texture			
Particle Type			
Description			

LOCATION 4

	SQUARE 10	SQUARE 11	SQUARE 12
Color			
Texture			
Particle Type			
Description			

From *Teaching Kids to Change the World: Lessons to Inspire Social Responsibility for Grades 6–12* by Jennifer Griffin-Wiesner, M.Ed., and Chris Maser, M.S. This page may be reproduced for educational, noncommercial uses only. Copyright © 2008 by Search Institute; 800-888-7828; www.search-institute.org.

location to location? From one another at the same location?

3. What might your observations mean about the environments to which these squares were exposed?

4. Who is responsible for the air quality at these locations? Why?

5. Who is affected by the quality of this air? Who is not affected?

6. How might one person's actions improve or worsen the quality of air that another person breathes?

LESSON 16

The World Is a Living Trust

Although it's common to speak of land stewardship, we prefer thinking of the whole world as a "living trust." A living trust is like a promise made by us today to safeguard something for the future. In making a promise, we relinquish a little personal freedom with the bond of our word.

In keeping our promise, we forfeit a bit of freedom because we limit some of our behaviors, but we do so for future gain. To break such a promise is to lose some of our integrity. The reason people hesitate to make promises lies in the uncertainty of tomorrow's circumstances. Helping quell the fear of uncertainty is the purpose of a living trust.

In a legal sense, a living trust is a transfer of property today, including the legal title, to an impartial caretaker or trustee. The living trust can consist of real property (such as a home or land) or personal property (such as livestock, jewelry, or interest in a business). The person who creates the trust (such as a land owner) can watch the trust operate, determine whether it fully satisfies his or her expectations, and can revoke or amend the trust as necessary.

Often, natural, human, and community resources are thought of as income or rev-enue, rather than as raw capital—as output, rather than input. But there needs to be an ongoing investment in order for a system, including any type of trust, to be sustainable. A trustee can be considered responsible only if he or she is committed to seeking and establishing ways to enhance the capital of the trust—not damaging, diminishing, or destroying it. We can enjoy fruit indefinitely from an apple tree, but only if the tree is nurtured and maintained with care. A living trust, then, is about the quality of life offered to future generations; it is not about the acquisition of possessions.

"Trusteeship" is the process of helping people learn to work together to address the common interests of all generations within the context of sustainability—biological, cultural, and economic. Remember, to protect the best of what we have in the present for the present and the future, we must continually change our thinking and our behavior. Society's saving grace is that we all have a choice in the matter. Whatever needs to be done can be—if enough people want it to be done and decide to do it.

ACTIVITY
BIG DIG

Purpose
For young people to see and consider that many of the things they leave behind in this world will remain for others to experience.

Materials
- Garden shovel
- An outdoor site for burying items
- Popsicle sticks
- Permanent marker
- Various items to test for decomposition

Preparation
Get permission to dig on the site where items will be buried. Look for a spot that will remain undisturbed during the experiment.

This activity works well across the span of several weeks to months or over the course of a school year.

Class Steps

1. Introduce the activity by talking about the natural process of decomposition.
2. Develop a system for describing the decomposition of the items you're going to bury. You might rate the decomposition of each item on a 1 to 5 scale, as follows:

   1 = All material is present and intact.
   2 = Material is soft and has a few holes.
   3 = About half the material is decomposed.
   4 = The material is largely decomposed and all that's left are scraps.
   5 = The material is completely decomposed.

3. Choose and obtain at least five different items to bury and test. Ideas include disposable diapers, paper or plastic plates and cups, paper or plastic bags, pens, paper, and pencils, and fresh and packaged food supplies.
4. Label one popsicle stick for each test item.
5. Bury your items where they will not be disturbed for at least three to six weeks or longer. Mark each burial spot with popsicle stick markers.
6. When the test period is up, dig up the material and record your observations and ratings on *Resource 12: Big Dig Observation Sheet* (page 47).

Follow-up Discussion

1. Describe what you found when you unearthed the test items.
2. What does this exercise tell you about what happens to things we leave behind for future generations?
3. What do you think would happen to these items if we left them in the ground for a year? Five years? 20? 50? 100? 2,000?
4. In today's world, what gifts and challenges do you see that were left behind by previous generations?
5. What gifts and challenges would you like to leave for the generations that come after you?

TAKING IT TO THE NEXT LEVEL
SUSTAINING A SYSTEM

Level 1
An important measure of a system's sustainability is the amount of time the system can continue circulating the energy within it. For a community's economy, this means keeping the same dollars circulating among various businesses and individuals within that community. Have class members list the local establishments that are owned by or employ people from your community. Encourage your students to spend their resources (such as the money they spend on food, clothing, and entertainment) in the neighborhood as much as possible.

Level 2
Ask students to keep a record of the money (every penny!) they earn and spend for two weeks. Then have students analyze their individual and class money management habits, using bar graphs or pie charts to show how they distributed their dollars. Ask students whether and how they would manage their money differently if they could do it a second time.

Level 3
Using information they have gathered about local or national plans for a particular policy change, help students draft an alternative plan to submit to their senators and representatives or local officials (for instance, campaign finance reform, universal health care, student and teacher accountability and testing measures, and so on). Use *Resource 13: All Sides Now—An Assessment Plan* (page 48) to develop a list of people who might be affected (positively or negatively) by your plan.

Big Dig Observation Sheet

Today's Date:

BURIAL DATE	ITEM	RATING	NOTES ON DECOMPOSITION

From *Teaching Kids to Change the World: Lessons to Inspire Social Responsibility for Grades 6–12* by Jennifer Griffin-Wiesner, M.Ed., and Chris Maser, M.S. This page may be reproduced for educational, noncommercial uses only. Copyright © 2008 by Search Institute; 800-888-7828; www.search-institute.org.

Rating Scale

1 = All material is present and intact.
2 = Material is soft and has a few holes.
3 = About half the material is decomposed.
4 = The material is largely decomposed and all that's left are scraps.
5 = The material is completely decomposed.

All Sides Now—
An Assessment Plan

The Issue:

PERSON/GROUP	WHY THEY HAVE AN INTEREST	HOW THE PLAN MAY AFFECT THEM

From *Teaching Kids to Change the World: Lessons to Inspire Social Responsibility for Grades 6–12* by Jennifer Griffin-Wiesner, M.Ed., and Chris Maser, M.S. This page may be reproduced for educational, noncommercial uses only. Copyright © 2008 by Search Institute; 800-888-7828; www.search-institute.org.

Relationships, Not Numbers, Keep Systems Sustainable

It is proof of a base and low mind for one to wish to think with the masses or majority, merely because the majority is the majority. Truth does not change because it is, or is not, believed by a majority of the people.

Giordano Bruno (1548–1600), Italian philosopher and cosmologist

Consider the old timber company slogan: We plant ten trees for every one we cut. No amount of newly planted seedlings can ever completely replace logged, mature trees that once constituted a viable forest in present space and time. It is the pattern of the trees' relationships to each other and to the landscape (in the form of interrelated habitats) that creates the stability in a forest. And so it is with commands in a computer program, words on a page, and the cells within our bodies: all are related in complex patterns to their surrounding elements.

LESSON 17

Self-Reinforcement— The Secret of Stable Systems

In the "stunning complexity" of the rain forest in Gabon, West Africa, independent field biologist Louise Emmons says, "You can stand anywhere and be surrounded by hundreds of organisms that are all 'doing something,' going about their living in countless interactions—ants carrying leaves, birds dancing, bats singing, giant blue wasps wrestling with giant tarantulas, caterpillars pretending they are bird droppings . . ."

Emmons found nine unique species of squirrels that all live together in one forest in Gabon. Each is a different size. Three species have specialized diets or habits, which leaves six more species that feed on nuts, fruits, and insects, and could therefore be potential competitors for food.

But a closer look reveals that three of the six species—one large, one medium, and one small—live exclusively in the canopy of the forest, where the largest one, a "giant" squirrel, feeds primarily on very large, hard nuts.

The smaller two squirrel species eat proportionally smaller fruits and nuts. The remaining three species—again, one large, one medium, and one small—live exclusively on the ground. These three squirrel species eat the same varieties of fruits and nuts as their neighbors in the canopy, but then only after fruits and nuts have fallen to the ground.

The forest in Gabon is evergreen. Fruit can be found on trees throughout the year, although any given tree species produces fruit for only a short period each year. To support three species of squirrels, eight species of monkeys, and eight species of fruit-eating bats (and more) in the rain forest canopy, the forest must have a wide variety of trees and lianas (high-climbing, usually woody vines), each of which produces fruits and nuts in its own rhythm. The varying sizes of fruits and nuts can support different sizes of squirrels with different tastes, and when these fruits and nuts fall to the ground, they can then feed the ground-foraging squirrel species.

If biodiversity is to be maintained, each individual tree must succeed in leaving offspring. Seeds and tender seedlings are among the richest foods available, and their succulence greatly increases their chances of being eaten by the large numbers of hungry animals searching for food around the bases of fruit- and nut-bearing trees. Similarly, organisms such as fungi, worms, and insects soon accumulate where seeds and seedlings are concentrated. The organisms spread from one seed or seedling to another.

Seeds that are carried away from such concentrations of hungry organisms are more likely to succeed in germinating. Another major benefit of seeds being carried away from the parent tree is the availability of a wide variety of places with different conditions into which a seed is likely to fall. A new condition might offer a pocket of better soil on a mound created by termites or in a spot where a dead tree has created a hole in the canopy that lets in sunlight.

It's no accident that roughly 80 to 95 percent of tree species in tropical rain forests produce fruits dispersed by birds and mammals. By dispersing seeds, birds and mammals maintain the rich diversity of tree species, an action that not only forms their habitat but also perpetuates it. This is an ideal example of a *self-reinforcing feedback loop*.

Many tree species in tropical rain forests, especially those that germinate in the dark understory, produce large seeds that carry enough stored energy to grow leaves and roots without much help from the sun. Such fruits and seeds are often so large that only similarly proportioned birds and mammals can swallow or carry them. In Gabon, for example, in the area studied by Emmons, monkeys dispersed 67 percent of the fruits eaten by animals.

Seed-dispersing animals, such as large birds and large monkeys, are critical to replacing the large trees and lianas of the forest canopy and thus helping them survive. However, these animals are the first to disappear when humans hunt for food. These species, along with elephants, have already been hunted so heavily that they have either been drastically reduced in numbers or eliminated completely over vast areas of the African forest.[5] A similar situation now exists with large birds and large monkeys in the tropical rain forests of Central and South America.

ACTIVITY

DASTARDLY DEVELOPMENT DEEDS

Purpose

For young people to sense what it might be like to have their habitat increasingly encroached upon over a period of time.

Materials
- Two index cards per person
- An empty one-gallon coffee can

Preparation

1. Set aside one blank card per person.

2. Next, count out enough cards to allow one for 3/4 of the students (do not use the remaining 1/4 of the cards). Write on these cards words that represent open spaces in the community where young people can enjoy the outdoors (such as parks, bike trails, picnic grounds, swimming pools, ball fields, playgrounds, and woods). Use terms that resonate with your students based on your community's characteristics.

3. Shuffle the blank and labeled cards, and place them in the container.

Class Steps

1. With students seated, ask each one to draw a card from the container.

2. Tell students who drew blank cards that you're sorry, but there is no safe outdoor place for them to hang out. They must put their cards back in the container and go home (sit against the wall) while the others enjoy the outdoors.

3. Explain that you've just learned that home developers are looking for new land to purchase in your community and are willing to pay a very good price. Tell the students who are still "playing outside" that they must put their cards back in the container.

4. Ask these students to draw a new card. Those who draw blank cards must join the others and sit against the wall.

5. Repeat as many times as seems effective, using a new reason each time. As students continue to drop out, ask all students to suggest reasons why public spaces become rare. Potential reasons for diminishing outdoor spaces might include:
   - Lakes become contaminated by illegally dumped chemical waste.
   - Developers want to turn open playing fields into golf courses, building sites, and other development projects.
   - Loggers cut down stands of trees in order to sell the lumber.
   - Trails are closed to the public because litter and other maintenance issues become a chronic problem.

Follow-up Discussion

1. How did it feel to control open space when others could not? To be denied open space when others had access?

2. When you learned that some open spaces would be taken away, how did you react?

3. In what ways does this exercise remind you of events that happen in your own community?

4. Who decides what natural resources are valuable and important in your community?

5. Do young people have a voice in your community? Why or why not?

6. How can you make your opinions known?

LESSON 18

Sustainability— It's About Effectiveness, Not Efficiency

We frequently confuse efficiency with effectiveness. The result is often an attempt to reduce and/or eliminate backup systems that may be considered inefficient, unnecessary, and not economical. In reality, backup systems are an important part of a system's composition, structure, function, and resiliency.

To understand the difference between efficiency and effectiveness, consider pine trees, which release abundant amounts of pollen carried great distances by air currents. Some of the pollen lands on pine seeds and cause new trees to germinate. Although an inefficient mode of pollination (many, many more grains of pollen are produced than ever fertilize available pine seeds), the pollination system is highly effective, as evidenced by the persistence of pine trees through the ages. And the "unneeded" grains of pollen are eaten by a variety of organisms, each of which benefits from the rich nutrient source. Nothing in nature is wasted. Waste, as people think of it, is an economic concept—not an ecological one.

Another aspect of the efficiency versus effectiveness dichotomy is the notion of backups versus redundancies. Backups are a fundamental feature of effective, sustainable systems.

Chris recalls a simple backup that was once essential to his comfort. While working in the deserts of Egypt, he spent two to three weeks at a time with only enough water for an occasional "spit bath." Showering was always a great pleasure upon returning to Cairo. In the early '60s, however, the city's water mains broke down regularly, shutting off water to faucets, toilets, and tubs.

The first time this happened to Chris, he was literally covered in soap. Nothing he tried could turn the water back on. Unable to rinse, Chris simply had to dry off the lather and put his clothes back on. He spent the next eight hours encased in sweaty, soapy, itchy film. During that time, Chris checked the faucet every fifteen to twenty minutes—each time desperately hoping water would flow, to no avail.

When the water supply eventually flowed again, Chris immediately filled the bathtub, turned on the shower, and rinsed thoroughly. Thereafter, he always filled the tub with rinse water, just in case the shower water shut off (which it occasionally did). And because he had set aside enough water in the tub as a backup, Chris was comfortable.

Today, we have access to many sophisticated backup systems, including the computer flash drive, a portable backup device that saves electronic data in a compact format, and the gasoline-powered electrical generator, which supplies electricity when the usual source is unexpectedly cut off. We also rely on simple backup systems, such as flashlights, candles, and wood-burning stoves, when electricity fails.

Built-in backup mechanisms give all types of systems the resilience to either resist change or bounce back after a disturbance. In this way, a backup system acts as an insurance policy that protects and ensures the continuation of a system after a major disruption. However, human communities often ignore the necessity for backup systems, despite the fact that they are essential to systems in nature.

With respect to ecosystems, each has built-in backup systems that contain more than one species capable of performing similar functions. Such backups give an ecosystem its resilience. Backup systems, in a biological sense, can be thought of as an environmental insurance policy.

Why do we ignore the value of backup systems? It's because we sometimes fail to grasp the subtle difference between an essential backup system and an unnecessary duplication or redundancy, mistakenly considering backups a waste of money. For example, although society's ever-increasing reliance on electricity makes us vulnerable to electrical blackouts, community power grids often rely on computers, eliminating the human, manual component, which is considered an unnecessary duplication or redundancy and thus a waste of money.

ACTIVITY
WHO IS BACKING YOU UP?

Purpose
For young people to learn that it's their right and their important responsibility to ask questions about backup plans that support the infrastructure of their school and other environments in which they live.

Materials
- Colored adhesive dots
- Chart paper and marker

Preparation

Prepare a story from your own experience that illustrates the importance of a contingency or backup plan.

Class Steps

1. Describe your own experience with a backup system. Ask students for examples of times when they've relied on backups (a "land line" telephone when electric cordless phones and cell phones don't work; public transportation when a car breaks down; candles or a portable generator for power outages; staying with a neighbor or an older sibling when parents aren't available).

2. Point out that it takes a lot of people and systems to keep your school running smoothly. Much of what goes on uses "behind the scenes" systems that students may never think about: infrastructure for water, heating, cooling, and plumbing; human systems for substitute teachers, bus drivers, cafeteria cooks, and so on.

3. As a class, brainstorm on paper a list of things that are needed to keep the school running in case of an unforeseen circumstance like an electrical blackout.

4. Give each student three dot stickers. Using the adhesive dots, ask students to vote on the school systems (and their backups) that they would like to learn more about.

5. Have students interview administrators, custodians, and teachers to learn more about the school backup systems that interest them most.

Follow-up Discussion

1. Did you learn anything during your interview that surprised you? If so, what?

2. How secure is your school in terms of its backup systems?

3. What actions would you like to take as a result of what you've learned?

LESSON 19

"Simple" Doesn't Always Equal "Better"

Imagine that your town's budget is shrinking. Suppose one of the guarantees your newly elected mayor made in order to win your vote was that he would balance the town budget. To keep this pledge, all that's necessary is to eliminate those services whose total budgets add up to the over-expenditure. Simple, isn't it?

Not exactly. What would happen, for example, if all police and fire services were eliminated? What difference would it make, assuming price was the same and the budget could still be balanced, if road and bridge maintenance was eliminated instead? Or how about closing and consolidating schools? The responsibility of town government may be simplified by eliminating services, but government functionality may also be compromised when essential services are no longer performed.

Fragile systems—those lacking a full complement of backup alternatives—can go awry in more ways than one, and can break down more suddenly and with less warning than robust systems. Fragile systems have a larger number of components with fewer backups than do robust ones, and the failure of any component can disrupt the system. Therefore, when a well-organized system is altered for human benefit, it is made more fragile, which means that more planning and maintenance are required to match the stability of the original system.

While sustainability means maintaining the critical functions performed by a system, it does not mean restoring or maintaining the original condition just as it was. To remove a piece of the whole may be acceptable, provided we know which piece is being removed, what that piece does, and what effect the loss of its function will have on the stability of the whole system. Otherwise, eliminating such a piece can result in unintended consequences.

ACTIVITY
THE WEB OF LIFE

Purpose
To help students understand the strength of a multifaceted infrastructure versus one that is simple.

Materials
- Five or more balls of different-colored yarn
- Several lightweight balls (such as beach balls)

Class Steps
1. Have students sit in a circle.
2. Explain that the balls of yarn represent different parts of an ecosystem: trees, plants, birds, mammals, insects, water, and so on. The beach balls represent people living within the system. (Alternatively, yarn balls could also represent parts of a community: schools, clinics, post office, doctors, dentists, water, phones, electricity, and so on.)
3. Give one person a ball of yarn.
4. Have the student hold the end of the yarn and throw the rest of the ball to someone else across the circle.
5. The next person should hold on to the thread and toss the rest of the ball to a third person.
6. Repeat until the yarn ball is completely unrolled. Then start the next ball of yarn (you can introduce more than one ball at a time if the group is large and the yarn-tossing doesn't get too chaotic). When all the yarn is unrolled, it should form a web.

7. Toss the beach balls onto the yarn web and have students bounce them around. Explain that while humans are a part of ecosystems, what's more important is that we are also dependent upon them.
8. Have students roll up one yarn ball at a time and name the part of the ecosystem they are "removing" (as the yarn is rolled up), such as "Let's take logs out of the area: remove the green yarn." Keep the beach balls bouncing all the while.
9. Beach balls will be harder and harder to keep aloft as the strands of yarn are removed.

Follow-up Discussion
1. How easy is it to support the "humans" (beach balls) when the yarn "ecosystem" is complete?
2. What happens when we start to simplify or take away various parts of the ecosystem?

TAKING IT TO THE NEXT LEVEL
RELATIONSHIPS, NOT NUMBERS, KEEP SYSTEMS STABLE

Level 1
Take a walking tour of your building's grounds. Notice and describe the balance between grass, concrete, gardens, trees, and other surfaces and vegetation. Have students find out who is responsible for maintaining these areas and how the maintenance is carried out. Is fertilizer required? Weed killer? Pruning or weeding? When rainwater runs off, where does it flow initially? And where does it end up?

Level 2
Read *Resource 14: A Garden Story* on page 56. Work with youth to develop a proposal for adding complexity to the grounds of your school or meeting place so that school grounds require less "control" and maintenance. Planting perennials, putting in rain gardens, and cre-

ating rock gardens are all ways to accomplish the goal.

Level 3

Help your students contact people in your community who are responsible for managing and caring for public open spaces. Prepare a list of interview questions regarding current open spaces, the plans and/or protections in place regarding those spaces, and the way decisions are made to maintain or change them. Interview as many people as possible. Based on what you learn, raise awareness of ecological practices in your community by preparing a letter to the editor or a guest column for your local paper.

A Garden Story

When Chris and his wife, Zane, bought their home, their lawn was a sorry sight, and the vegetable garden was merely a gigantic patch of weeds. A few forgotten flowers were scattered at random. Had the two been content with this haphazard arrangement, their yard might have been considered relatively maintenance-free, aside from an occasional mowing. However, they intended to live there for many years, which led them to have a vastly different outlook on their garden and yard and its considerable potential.

Chris and Zane spent months sitting in, looking at, and walking around their unkempt patch of earth until they formed a vision of what they eventually wanted it to look like. The more they groomed the garden, the more specialized their flower and vegetable beds became, and, as a result, the more fragile the internally functioning ecosystem became as the gardeners began to alter the naturally self-sustaining cycle of soil enrichment. As the fragility of the garden's ecosystem increased, so did the amount of time and energy that was required to maintain the deliberate processes that were disrupted by designing gardens that were pleasing to their senses.

Weeding disrupts the natural recycling of organic material, which nourishes the soil and governs the biological balance among soil microorganisms. To understand the importance of the disruption (removing weeds from the area), it first helps to understand the function of a weed—a plant that generally grows where you don't want it to grow. The weeds in Chris's garden were an important source of organic material created from the interaction of plants, sunlight, carbon dioxide, chemical elements, and water.

When weeds die, the organic matter enters the soil, where it becomes a source of energy for bacterial organisms already present in the soil. These organisms are needed to break down plant material and maintain the health of the soil. Weeds serve a vital function in the creation of healthy soil, and weeding disrupts that function.

Chris realized he had to deliberately add composted organic material to the garden soil in order to replace nutrient-producing processes otherwise performed naturally by the weeds he had eliminated in his quest to maintain a desired sense of order. Chris discovered that the more intentionally he tried to control his gardens, the more intensely he had to control his gardens to maintain what he had created—the self-reinforcing feedback loop that every gardener creates, to one degree or another, through the act of gardening.

From *Teaching Kids to Change the World: Lessons to Inspire Social Responsibility for Grades 6–12* by Jennifer Griffin-Wiesner, M.Ed., and Chris Maser, M.S. This page may be reproduced for educational, noncommercial uses only. Copyright © 2008 by Search Institute; 800-888-7828; www.search-institute.org.

We Can Only Manage Ourselves

When I despair, I remember that all through history the ways of truth and love have always won. There have been tyrants, and murderers, and for a time they can seem invincible, but in the end they always fall. Think of it—always.

Mohandas K. Gandhi (1869–1948), Indian political and spiritual leader

Sustainability depends upon the notion of a shared belief in human equality. The practical expression of this belief means that all people pledge to defend the rights of the individual, and each person pledges to defend the rights of all—the concept of all for one and one for all. We begin by learning to listen respectfully to one another's ideas. While it's sometimes wise to "agree to disagree," it's also important not to jump to conclusions, accepting that each of us is initially limited by our individual experiences and perceptions of the same event.

When these things happen, we engage in the most fundamental aspects of democracy. We can draw conclusions and make decisions by talking, listening, understanding, compromising, agreeing, and keeping agreements in an honorable way.

LESSON 20

Democracy Nurtures Sustainability

A central principle of sustainability is to live by the honest practice of democracy. Then connection, sharing, compassion, accep-

tance, tolerance, honesty, and the concept of "innocent until proven guilty" become central to a society's viability.

Democracy is a system of shared power, consisting of checks and balances in which individuals can equally affect the outcome of political decisions. It is a system designed to protect individual freedoms within socially acceptable relationships, allowing people to live peacefully with one another, individually and collectively.

For our democracy to survive, we must give young people a voice and empower them to use it to ensure that the earth, as a living trust, endures through the present age into the future. Otherwise, a single decision made unilaterally today, without consideration for future generations, leads to another and another, and begins a cycle that silences or ignores the voices of children who are our legacy.

ACTIVITY
LITTLE STEPS ADD UP TO BIG CHANGES

Purpose
For young people to understand that their individual actions, when combined with the actions of others who share their beliefs and passions, can have a significant impact.

Materials
- Copies of *Resource 15: The Bald Eagle* (page 59)

Preparation
Plan ahead for students to talk about endangered species with a school or community librarian (or other school or community expert).

Class Steps
1. Read *Resource 15: The Bald Eagle* to your students.
2. Explain to young people that, as a class, you are going to choose by majority vote one endangered animal and one action to take on behalf of that animal.
3. Ask for suggestions and include some of your own (e.g., the spotted owl, snowy owl, American bison, and Canada lynx).
4. Allow for brief discussion, followed by a vote.
5. Help young people research the endan-

gered species, including government and community actions, sources of the endangerment, and proposed remedies.

Follow-up Discussion
1. Ask students to determine one or more positive actions they can take on behalf of their chosen species.
2. They can write letters to the state Department of Natural Resources, sponsor a resolution to be adopted by their local or state government and present it to representatives, educate their parents about the issue, or invite another class to hear them make a presentation on the endangered species.

LESSON 21
We Always Have Choices

In life, we always have choices—with a few notable exceptions. For instance, we can't:

- Not make choices during our lifetime;
- Experience absolute freedom;
- Do something that has no consequences;
- Reverse the effects of what we do; or
- Choose not to die.

These exceptions aside, we have choices to make in how we live—and we must choose. If we don't like the outcome, we may have the option of choosing again. We become the products of the consequences of our choices. We continually reap the harvest of what we sow, although we cannot always choose the timing, as that requires absolute freedom, which doesn't exist in our interdependent world.

The challenge for most people is to choose between two equally valid options. To choose one direction is to accept whatever lies ahead and give up the direction another choice would have brought. Because our lives unfold before us as we live them, our dilemma is that we lack a well-marked road map by which to navigate.

The Bald Eagle

A vision without a task is but a dream. A task without a vision is drudgery.
A vision and a task are the hope of the world.
FROM A CARVING ON A CHURCH IN SUSSEX, ENGLAND

A vision, like the sustainability of a community, is a perpetual work in progress; it captures the ideal, the utopia, that people seek.

Bald eagles are a symbol of dignity, power, and pride in the United States. Many Native Americans consider them sacred. And they are a fine example of what happens when vision and action come together. However, since its adoption in 1782 by the U.S. Congress as the nation's emblem, the bald eagle has had a rocky existence. At that time, its numbers were estimated at between 25,000 and 75,000 in the continental United States.

As the human population increased, eagles faced numerous threats, including loss of habitat, illegal killing for trophy hunting or protection of livestock, and the pesticide DDT, which was sprayed on crops and contaminated water plants and wildlife upon which eagles feed. DDT weakened the bird's eggshells, causing them to break during incubation.

Although Congress passed the Bald Eagle Protection Act in 1940, by the mid-1900s the bald eagle population in the continental United States was thought to be fewer than 450 nesting pairs.

Then in 1962, environmentalist Rachel Carson wrote *Silent Spring*, a courageous book that was the first to draw attention to the risks of long-term pesticide use and misuse. There was no "quick fix" for the damage done to bald eagles and other birds of prey, but a shared vision regarding the importance of saving them led to a series of decisions and actions that began to collectively turn the tide toward protection.

Ten years later, DDT use was banned in the U.S. In 1973, Congress passed the Endangered Species Act, with the bald eagle immediately being listed. The U.S. Fish and Wildlife Service also initiated a captive breeding and reintroduction program. In the 1980s, the use of lead shot was banned in waterfowl hunting, reducing the likelihood of eagles becoming poisoned by eating hunter-killed or -injured birds.

Today in North America, there may be close to 100,000 of these remarkable birds in the wild—and, as of June 2007, they have been officially removed from the list of endangered species.

From *Teaching Kids to Change the World: Lessons to Inspire Social Responsibility for Grades 6–12* by Jennifer Griffin-Wiesner, M.Ed., and Chris Maser, M.S. This page may be reproduced for educational, noncommercial uses only. Copyright © 2008 by Search Institute; 800-888-7828; www.search-institute.org.

In this manner, we're much like the ancient sailors for whom sailing was a complicated endeavor, because navigation involved observing the angle of the sun and the position of the stars using astrolabe, sextant, and compass. While these instruments could tell mariners in which direction they were already headed, they needed to actually see the celestial bodies to determine which way to go to reach their destination. And one of the mariners' challenges was in accurately measuring elapsed time so they could also measure their movement relative to the stars and planets and determine the speed of their ship. The invention of the mechanical clock greatly increased the predictability of their travel, but it still could not predict what lay ahead.

While there are no absolutely predictable outcomes to the choices we make in life, unpredictability does not preclude the fact that we must still make choices. As uncomfortable as potential choices and their outcomes may be at times, the necessity of choosing is the price of free will.

ACTIVITY

ON THE ROAD TO SOMEWHERE

Purpose

To illustrate that all situations require us to make choices, whether we do so intentionally and thoughtfully or not.

Materials

- A playground or open field

Class Steps

1. Bring the class to a large field or playground.
2. Have students stand at one point, and explain that their job for the next 5–10 minutes is to get from where they are standing (Point A) to another point you have chosen ahead of time (Point B).
3. Use a quick system to divide the class into three groups.

4. Tell the first group they can take any route they choose to reach Point B, but they must go together as a group.
5. Tell the second group they can wander wherever they choose, observing the landscape around them and what they see on the ground and in the neighborhood as they walk toward Point B.
6. Tell the third group they must travel together slowly in a perfectly straight line, ending at Point B.
7. Once each group has reached Point B, regroup and debrief.

Follow-up Discussion

1. Did your group follow instructions exactly as given? Why or why not?
2. What did you observe and think about in traveling from Point A to Point B?
3. How did the experiences of your group compare to those of the other groups?
4. What choices did you all make in arriving at your destination?
5. Did any of you have the option of not making choices? Explain.
6. What does this tell you about making choices in everyday life?

LESSON 22

We Become What We Oppose When We React Instead of Responding

"What you are stands over you the while, and thunders so that I cannot hear what you say to the contrary," Ralph Waldo Emerson wrote in his 1876 essay "Social Aims." Emerson might easily have been speaking of hatred and prejudice, attitudes that have the power to control our lives in spite of our protests to the contrary.

As long as old hatreds are carried forward from one generation to the next, war, terrorism, and other forms of violence will continue. We are destined to repeat acts of hatred and violence until people let go of old ways of thinking and reacting. When we can do so, we will be able to experience the transformative possibilities of the present, and thereby make the best use of precious human talent, money, and irreplaceable natural resources that allow us to enrich, rather than impoverish, each succeeding generation.

Through experiencing the consequences of our actions, we can learn the difference between reacting and responding. We react spontaneously, sometimes out of insecurity and a perceived need for self-defense and retaliation, becoming the very thing that we oppose. Can we learn to respond intentionally to one another with trust inspired by acceptance, and transform fear and hatred into compassion and justice?

If you consider that happy, positive, loving thoughts are often described as feeling light, and that angry, negative, and fearful thoughts are like heavy weights, you can test the difference between the two by paying attention to the relative weight of your own thoughts as they are affected by circumstances.

Think back to a time when someone with a sour attitude entered a room filled with happy people. What happened to the energy in the room? Remember also a time when an effervescent person entered a room full of predominantly dour people. Again, what happened to the energy in the room? The levity of one person's thoughts can electrify a room full of people just as the morose thoughts of another person can drag those same people into subdued seriousness.

Understanding the power of human thought to affect collective energy is critical, because the psychological balance of society is determined by the weight of individual thought. While a thought of love is but a feather's weight, when placed on the social and environmental scale its lasting effect outweighs by a hundredfold a thought of fear. It is, therefore, by our thoughts that we can affect the world we live in—for good or ill.

Consider a story from Africa: A boy wanted to give his teacher a gift, but he was very poor. So he walked two miles to the beach and picked up a handful of pink sand. He then walked two miles back. The next day he gave the sand to his teacher.

She thanked him for the beautiful sand, and said, "But you walked so far."

"The journey," he replied, "is part of the gift."

We hope it is clear that each time we, as individuals, express a positive thought, one consciously conceived in optimism and hope, we counter the negative side of the scale. Today, more than ever, the future of our earth depends on how we choose to think and act, because it's by our thoughts that we create the legacy we bequeath to present and future generations.

ACTIVITY
MOVING ENERGY

Purpose
To create for the students a metaphor for the energy of their thoughts and their respective outcomes.

Materials
- Extendable, spring-loaded curtain rod
- A large piece of cloth or curtain panel (large enough to block air movement)

Preparation
Position the rod and curtain across the top of a hallway or doorway.

Class Steps
1. Have one student at a time walk swiftly (as if angry) toward the curtain and then stride away from it. What happens to the curtain?
2. Next, have each student approach the curtain slowly and gently (as if peaceful), and walk away from it equally calmly. What happens this time?

3. Now, have students approach the curtain, one at a time, turn their backs to it, and let the curtain settle down. What happens?

Follow-up Discussion

1. As always, the way we behave is our choice. That choice affects the circumstances that follow, setting in motion an ongoing series of reactions or responses.
2. What does this experience teach you about your attitude?
3. Do you think this experience will help you control your attitude in the future when things don't go the way you want them to? Why or why not?
4. How will this experience affect the way you treat other people and/or animals?

LESSON 23
Acceptance Is the Key

In the late 1990s, Jennifer participated in a series of workshops that brought together religious education specialists from Christian, Jewish, Muslim, and Baha'i faith communities across the country. There were clear differences in the practices and beliefs across and within these broad faith traditions, which was to be expected. But, as the workshop participants, other leaders, and Jennifer discovered, there were also tremendous similarities in shared values and, most important, in a sincere longing to understand and really know one another.

The project coordinators provided training in best practices to help young people develop their faith, learn to get along with one another, and work together. Participants were also given safe, comfortable environments in which to socialize, share ideas, and learn from one another. The positive response was overwhelming.

Participants began meeting on their own, one-on-one and in groups. Some chose to bring together young people, too. One group traveled together cross-country to participate in an interfaith Habitat for Humanity building project. They learned that when they moved beyond merely tolerating one another to truly accepting differences in each other, it allowed them all to be who and what they were. That kind of acceptance can bring wonderful and remarkable gifts into all our lives.

ACTIVITY
INSIDE OUT

Purpose

To help students understand that they are more alike than they are different by exploring examples of inclusion and exclusion.

Materials

• One chair for each participant

Preparation

Place chairs in a circle, leaving room to walk between each one.

Class Steps

1. Invite students to sit in the circle of chairs.
2. Tell them you'll read a statement and their job is to listen, think, and then follow the directions. Pause after each statement to give students time to respond and notice where others choose to stand. Read the following statements, modifying and adding to them as it seems appropriate:
   • If you've ever felt you were treated unfairly because of your gender, stand outside the circle.
   • If you've ever felt welcomed by a group of people you didn't even know, stand inside the circle.
   • If you've ever felt afraid for your personal safety because of your race, stand outside the circle.
   • If you have a friend of another racial,

cultural, or ethnic background, stand inside the circle.

- If you've ever felt you were treated unfairly because of your accent or your language, stand outside the circle.
- If you speak more than one language, stand inside the circle.
- If you've ever felt you were treated unfairly because of your body shape or size, stand outside the circle.
- If you've ever introduced yourself to someone you didn't know, stand inside the circle.
- Add other statements as you wish.

3. After you finish reading the statements, have students stay in the circle and discuss the following questions.

Follow-up Discussion

1. What surprised you about this activity? Did anything make you uncomfortable or sad? Relieved, proud, or admiring?
2. How does it feel to be labeled and treated according to that label? What assumptions do people make every day in our schools and communities?
3. What does this experience teach you about the power of words and ideas? How can words be used to make a positive difference?
4. Why is it easier sometimes to think about people's differences, rather than their similarities?
5. What difference do positive and negative attitudes make in our society? What lessons can you take away from this exercise that will help you in your daily interactions?

Adapted and reprinted with permission from *Make a World of Difference* by Dawn C. Oparah (Search Institute, 2006).

A Wise Response Depends on Reflection

Much has been written through the centuries about Utopia—that mythic place where people love one another, work is transformed into a labor of love or play, and social and environmental problems are untangled with patience, compassion, and ease. Our earth, too, could be like this, if only . . .

The difficulty with utopias is not that they are imagined perfection but rather that they are imagined cures for imperfection. Utopia is conceived of as a solution in an attempt to move away from an unwanted, negative circumstance, rather than as a goal to move toward.

To heal and protect a community, society, or other environment in a sustainable condition, we must have a destination toward which to journey. The ideal can then help define an agenda that rests firmly on the bedrock of a shared vision, one that incorporates the collective wisdom, personal courage, and political will needed to inspire true social progress. It requires only a choice and the determination to carry it out. Remember that failure is a crisis of will and imagination, not of possibilities. The only real failure lies in not taking risks, for without risks there can be no gains. In fact, success or failure is not the event itself but rather its interpretation.

ACTIVITY
CLASSROOM UTOPIA

Purpose
For young people to experience the possibility of creating the environment they hope for when their objectives are framed positively and they are committed to putting those objectives into practice.

Class Steps
1. Ask students to help you brainstorm the

best possible classroom they can imagine. Write down all their suggestions, phrasing them in the positive ("We'll all use kind words toward one another") and not the negative ("No name-calling").

2. Once you've made the list, ask students if there's anything on the list they think is impossible to make happen in the classroom. If yes, discuss why, whether you could alter the goal slightly to make it possible, and whether it's really needed in order to create the best possible classroom.

3. Tell the class that, together, you are all going to be intentional about making these things happen as often as possible.

4. Each person (including you) should sign the sheet. Post the sheet in the classroom as a reminder of your best intentions.

Follow-up Discussion

1. Check regularly on how things are going.
2. Ask:
   - What behaviors are helping us maintain our positive classroom atmosphere?
   - What behaviors detract from a positive atmosphere?
   - What can we do to have our classroom be just the way we hope it will be?

This activity is adapted with permission from the Southern Poverty Law Center's "Teaching Tolerance" Web site. For more information, see www.tolerance.org.

LESSON 25

You Can *Always* Start Today

The Daffodil Principle, by author Jaroldeen Edwards, tells of one person's effort to change the world, one small step at a time. A young woman repeatedly calls to invite her mother to "see the daffodils before they are over." Each time, the mother resists or delays making the visit. Eventually, the daughter does convince her mother to visit the acres of blooms in the San Bernardino Mountains. As they pull up to the gardens, the mother is astounded. There are five acres of flowers. "Who did this?" she asks. "Just one woman," replies her daughter. "She lives on the property. That's her home."

On the patio, a poster reads, "Answers to the Questions I Know You Are Asking:
   "50,000 bulbs.
   "One at a time, by one woman. Two hands, two feet, and one brain.
   "Begun in 1958."

The older woman is momentarily saddened in the face of such a tremendous, patient accomplishment. She muses about all the things she could have done, had she only started earlier, until her daughter matter-of-factly reminds her that it's *never* too late to begin. The important thing is to use the "Daffodil Principle"—get started!

ACTIVITY

WINDSHIELD TOUR

Purpose

For young people and the adults in their lives to carefully examine the challenges and resources in their community, and to better understand how they can make it a healthier, more positive place to live.

Note: A windshield tour can take many forms: parent-child pairs can do it on their own, multiple families can work together, and students and teacher can walk or ride a city bus.

Materials

- Copies of *Resource 16: Through the Windshield* (page 66) and a pen or pencil for each student
- Permission slips for each student (if applicable)

Preparation

Prepare and distribute permission slips to

parents and guardians if your group uses transportation and goes off-site. Secure chaperones and drivers, if necessary.

Class Steps

1. Tour your community (school neighborhood, students' home neighborhoods, your town or city) on foot, by bus, or car.
2. What are your community's strengths (green space for recreation, thriving businesses, good schools, new home construction, senior housing, community meeting space)?
3. What community weaknesses cause you concern (air pollution, panhandling, litter, lack of appropriate places for young people to hang out, violence)?
4. On *Resource 16: Through the Windshield*, record what you see, hear, smell, taste, and feel on your tour. Compare and contrast those experiences in your classroom discussion.

Follow-up Discussion

1. What stood out in your tour of the community?
2. What differences and similarities were there between what you observed and what adults (teachers or parents) noticed?
3. What do you think of your community after doing this exercise?
4. What things about the community would you like to change?
5. What good things are happening that you'd like to continue or build upon?
6. What action can you start today that will make the community better and more beautiful in the long run?

Adapted with permission from *Generators: 20 Activities to Recharge Your Intergenerational Group* by Jennifer Griffin-Wiesner (Search Institute, 2005).

WE CAN ONLY MANAGE OURSELVES

Level 1

As a class, choose a simple action that will make your school look or feel warmer or more beautiful, inside or out. It doesn't have to be complicated to be effective. Start today!

Level 2

Together with your students, identify a common concern or shared interest in your community. Help your group join or organize a walk-a-thon, fun run, bike-a-thon, or lap swim fund-raiser or rally that will benefit your community.

Level 3

Help students gather names and addresses of local elected decision makers (mayor, city council or school board, state representatives) who are in a position to influence a community concern. Acting as an adviser, help students organize and invite officials to participate in a speakers' forum or debate that involves a variety of perspectives. Have students research the issue in detail and prepare questions and commentary in advance. Students should serve as hosts, moderators, and even as participants in the forum. Invite the local press to provide coverage.

Through the Windshield

COMMUNITY STRENGTHS	COMMUNITY CONCERNS	COMMUNITY NEEDS
ADULTS SEE...	ADULTS SEE...	ADULTS SEE...

COMMUNITY STRENGTHS	COMMUNITY CONCERNS	COMMUNITY NEEDS
YOUTH SEE...	YOUTH SEE...	YOUTH SEE...

Reprinted with permission from *Step by Step! A Young Person's Guide to Positive Community Change* by The Mosaic Youth Center Board of Directors with Jennifer Griffin-Wiesner (Search Institute, 2001). From *Teaching Kids to Change the World: Lessons to Inspire Social Responsibility for Grades 6–12* by Jennifer Griffin-Wiesner, M.Ed., and Chris Maser, M.S. This page may be reproduced for educational, noncommercial uses only. Copyright © 2008 by Search Institute; 800-888-7828; www.search-institute.org.

True Sustainability Requires a Shared Vision

*A hundred times every day I remind myself that my inner
and outer life depend upon the labors of other men,
living and dead, and that I must exert myself in order to give in
the measure as I have received and am still receiving.*

Albert Einstein (1879–1955), German physicist

IN Monroe County, New York, high school students envisioned a welcoming school environment.[6] A 12th grader suggested that senior citizens in the community might want to volunteer to be morning greeters at their school if he and his classmates were willing to spring for coffee and doughnuts. He challenged a local group working to build Developmental Assets in the community to help the students coordinate their plan—and it worked.

When a community shares a vision of a sustainable future, it creates confidence, consensus, and energy in equal parts. At a deeper level, the vision engages our imagination and helps ferret out the questions that need to be asked, how they need to be phrased, and when it is appropriate to ask them. A community's shared vision is also preemptive conflict resolution.

By engaging young people's beginners' minds—filled with enthusiasm and a sense of possibility—through countless small-scale initiatives, people who are concerned with the health of their environment and with social justice can create an opportunity for a more positive, sustainable future. Imagination, as Albert Einstein noted, is more important than knowledge, and is the most powerful tool for social change.

But it also requires tenacity of purpose and persistence of action; otherwise, as Calvin Coolidge remarked, imagination is all but useless. "Nothing in the world can take the place of persistence. Talent will not; nothing is more common than unsuccessful [people] with talent. Genius will not; unrewarded genius is almost a proverb. Education will not; the world is full of educated derelicts. Persistence and determination alone are omnipotent."

LESSON 26

Shared Vision Is a Necessity

Ask a friend about his future and he might respond in terms of his vision, as in "I see myself running a marathon in five years" or "I want to operate my own business" and so on. You may hear of leaders, artists, and scientists who are described as visionaries. Similarly, schools, organizations, and even individuals often create vision or mission statements, which they use to help explain the work they do or want to do and how they will do it.

There is so much talk about vision—it must be important to have a vision, to be visionary, to be able to see further ahead, rather than just one step in front of the next. So, what does "having a vision" mean in practical terms? How do you, as a teacher, help your students create a vision?

Dag Hammarskjöld, former Secretary General of the United Nations, noted that "only he who keeps his eye fixed on the far horizon will find his right road." Having a vision means looking ahead to where you want to go, and letting that image guide you there. To us, having a vision also means having a strong organizing context built around interpersonal relationships—in the present, for the present and the future.

Consider the human body as an illustration of what we mean. As part of a highly organized context, each component of the body has a specific job or task that, when performed properly, keeps the entire body healthy.

When, for example, cancer cells are introduced into the body of a healthy animal, they may return to a normal functional pattern under the influence of the healthy body's powerful organizing context (the immune system). If, however, cancer cells stay too long without the guidance of a strong organizing context, they reach a point when they can

no longer be guided at all and become "rogue" cells in the new environment.

It is not surprising that the various parts of a system tend to lose focus when their context is disorganized or confused, whether they're part of a human body, the body of a human community, the body politic, or the body of humanity as a whole. The longer disorganization exists, the more difficult it is to reverse the effects; hence a community's need for the strong organizing context of a shared vision.

A shared vision has some distinctive traits. It:

- Tends to focus on a wide range of human concerns;
- Is strongly centered on the community;
- Can use alternative scenarios to explore a possible future by depicting in words and images what a community is striving to become;
- Relies on the trust, respect, and inclusion of interpersonal relationships;
- Is ideally suited to, and depends on, public involvement; and
- Is ideally suited to the use of creative, graphic imagery.

Although a shared vision does not replace other kinds of planning, it is the organizational context within which all other planning fits.

More than 3,000 years ago, Indian sages gave humanity one of the earliest spiritual writings, the Rig Veda. In it is an injunction that is the heart and soul of a shared vision:

Meet together, talk together:

May your minds comprehend alike:

Common be your action and achievement:

Common be your thoughts and intentions:

Common be the wishes of your heart

So there may be thorough union among you.

UNTANGLED UNITY

Purpose

For young people to experience the difference between working on a group problem when all are doing their own thing and when there is a shared vision for how to proceed.

Class Steps

1. Divide the class into two groups, A and B (or choose your own labels).
2. Ask each group to form a circle as far apart from one another as possible, but within hearing range of you (stand between the groups).
3. Instruct the students to extend their right hands and grasp the right hand of one other person in the circle, but not the person standing next to them.
4. Repeat step 3, this time grasping the left hand of a different person, again not an immediate neighbor.
5. Tell the groups that their task is to untangle themselves, without letting go of hands. They will need to move under, over, and through the spaces created by the arms and hands of those around them.
6. Then tell them that group A can talk while they do the exercise, but group B must be silent. If there is a particularly high level of trust in the class, you can also tell group B members to close their eyes.
7. Give each group enough time to either untangle themselves or give up in frustration. Circulate while they do this, offering encouragement and reminding group B to be silent.
8. Monitor their frustration level. If it's too high, let them open their eyes and talk to complete the exercise.

Follow-up Discussion

1. What was it like doing the activity in silence? How did it work? What did you notice?
2. What was it like doing the activity while being able to discuss it with others in the circle? How did it work? What did you notice?
3. What does this activity tell you about the benefit of having a "shared vision" of what you want and how you'll get there?
4. What happens in a community or group when no person can talk to another (or see another's perspective)?

TAKING IT TO THE NEXT LEVEL
TRUE SUSTAINABILITY REQUIRES A SHARED VISION

Level 1

Review the mission or vision statements of several organizations or agencies in your community. Your community may have its own vision statement.

Level 2

Have your students write an impromptu essay on the rights and responsibilities of living in a democracy.

Level 3

Use these steps to create a vision statement:

1. Invite group members to dream about the best-case scenario for an issue or topic you have talked about in the past.
2. Ask: If you were going to give a presentation about this vision, what would you say?
3. Ask participants to draw pictures of or write down their descriptions of the vision.
4. Invite each person to share her or his vision statement.
5. Make a list of key words, phrases, or images. Sort the words, phrases, and images into several key themes.
6. Ask each person to indicate her or his top five priorities by "starring" the

words, phrases, and images. Each can give five stars for her or his first priority, four stars for the second priority, and so on.

7. Have each student tally the stars and choose the top three to five items to create your group's vision statement.

As you complete the seven steps, use these techniques for keeping the process on track:

- Encourage individuals to think big and to dream about what they'd really love to be a part of—even if it doesn't feel practical.

- Start with brainstorming. Don't openly critique any of the ideas (and try not to judge them in your mind). Write them all down.

- Take a positive approach. Focus on opportunities, rather than obstacles or problems. Identify what you want, not what you don't want.

- Work to articulate your vision in simple terms. Keep it between 25 and 40 words.

Reprinted with permission from *The Journey of Community Change* by Jennifer Griffin-Wiesner (Search Institute, 2005).

Epilogue: Teaching Kids to Change the World—From Vision to Reality

Teaching young people to be part of creating and sustaining a vision for the future of our communities and our world requires self-determination, courage, and a letting go of fear. At its center, this vision cannot and will not be about preservation, but rather about doing the best we can to honorably push the limits of human possibility.

Pushing the limits of human possibility is a necessary condition of social evolution because, as Albert Einstein noted, "No problem can be solved from the same consciousness that created it." This captures both a compelling need for, as well as the significant challenges posed by, engaging young people in caring for the living trust we call Planet Earth.

If we want to live in a future of positive social quality and equality, we must change our unsustainable values and habits—and be determined and persistent in that change. We must also make sure that what we do is socially inclusive, which means that humanity must be physically and psychologically prepared for the opportunities and responsibilities that emerge as a result of people's growing interdependence.

Winston Churchill observed prior to England's entry into World War II that people avoid uncomfortable situations until it is too late to effectively confront them. If we can instead view change as a condition to be embraced, uncomfortable as it may be, then we have the hope of working toward and achieving a positive, sustainable future together.

It is possible to develop the attitudes, values, knowledge, and skills necessary to shape our own communities on all levels so that each reflects the principles of love, justice, equality, unity, and social and environmental sustainability. Educating our youth is crucial; we must encourage thinking in terms of historical processes and the inexorable movement toward a world civilization of ever-increasing consciousness, a movement whose successes are the legacy of all people and whose challenges belong increasingly to one world society.

A shared vision of a sustainable future must therefore be both ecologically and economically sound if it is going to enable people to think differently about their lives, and in so doing start to change them. The change must be for and about the people themselves. If it does not have a human face from which core human values shine, it will fail.

The process of implementing a shared vision is equivalent to negotiating a series of obstacles. Some constraints, such as those imposed by nature, are ecological and nonnegotiable. Although they can be—and often have been—circumvented, such circumvention has exacted an enormous cost in both human and environmental terms.

In contrast, other constraints (social, political, and economic) are negotiable. A community's vision of a sustainable future can be achieved by people who are committed to accepting the constraints imposed by nature and renegotiating those imposed by society. We are confident that, in the end, it will be the young people of this world who will lead the way in making this vision a reality.

40 Developmental Assets for Adolescents
(ages 12 to 18)

Search Institute has identified the following building blocks of healthy development — known as Developmental Assets— that help young people grow up healthy, caring, and responsible.

EXTERNAL ASSETS

Support

1. *Family Support*—Family life provides high levels of love and support.
2. *Positive Family Communication*—Young person and her or his parent(s) communicate positively, and young person is willing to seek advice and counsel from parent(s).
3. *Other Adult Relationships*—Young person receives support from three or more nonparent adults.
4. *Caring Neighborhood*—Young person experiences caring neighbors.
5. *Caring School Climate*—School provides a caring, encouraging environment.
6. *Parent Involvement in Schooling*—Parent(s) are actively involved in helping young person succeed in school.

Empowerment

7. *Community Values Youth*—Young person perceives that adults in the community value youth.
8. *Youth as Resources*—Young people are given useful roles in the community.
9. *Service to Others*—Young person serves in the community one hour or more per week.
10. *Safety*—Young person feels safe at home, at school, and in the neighborhood.

Boundaries and Expectations

11. *Family Boundaries*—Family has clear rules and consequences and monitors the young person's whereabouts.
12. *School Boundaries*—School provides clear rules and consequences.
13. *Neighborhood Boundaries*—Neighbors take responsibility for monitoring young people's behavior.
14. *Adult Role Models*—Parent(s) and other adults model positive, responsible behavior.
15. *Positive Peer Influence*—Young person's best friends model responsible behavior.
16. *High Expectations*—Both parent(s) and teachers encourage the young person to do well.

Constructive Use of Time

17. *Creative Activities*—Young person spends three or more hours per week in lessons or practice in music, theater, or other arts.
18. *Youth Programs*—Young person spends three or more hours per week in sports, clubs, or organizations at school and/or in the community.

19. *Religious Community*—Young person spends one or more hours per week in activities in a religious institution.
20. *Time at Home*—Young person is out with friends "with nothing special to do" two or fewer nights per week.

Commitment to Learning

21. *Achievement Motivation*—Young person is motivated to do well in school.
22. *School Engagement*—Young person is actively engaged in learning.
23. *Homework*—Young person reports doing at least one hour of homework every school day.
24. *Bonding to School*—Young person cares about her or his school.
25. *Reading for Pleasure*—Young person reads for pleasure three or more hours per week.

Positive Values

26. *Caring*—Young person places high value on helping other people.
27. *Equality and Social Justice*—Young person places high value on promoting equality and reducing hunger and poverty.
28. *Integrity*—Young person acts on convictions and stands up for her or his beliefs.
29. *Honesty*—Young person "tells the truth even when it is not easy."
30. *Responsibility*—Young person accepts and takes personal responsibility.
31. *Restraint*—Young person believes it is important not to be sexually active or to use alcohol or other drugs.

Social Competencies

32. *Planning and Decision Making*—Young person knows how to plan ahead and make choices.
33. *Interpersonal Competence*—Young person has empathy, sensitivity, and friendship skills.
34. *Cultural Competence*—Young person has knowledge of and comfort with people of different cultural/racial/ethnic backgrounds.
35. *Resistance Skills*—Young person can resist negative peer pressure and dangerous situations.
36. *Peaceful Conflict Resolution*—Young person seeks to resolve conflict nonviolently.

Positive Identity

37. *Personal Power*—Young person feels he or she has control over "things that happen to me."
38. *Self-Esteem*—Young person reports having a high self-esteem.
39. *Sense of Purpose*—Young person reports that "my life has a purpose."
40. *Positive View of Personal Future*—Young person is optimistic about her or his personal future.

This page may be reproduced for educational, noncommercial uses only. Copyright © 1997, 2006 by Search Institute; 800-888-7828; www.search-institute.org. All Rights Reserved.

Web Resources

Check out the following organizations and their Web sites for useful readings, curriculum ideas, background materials, tips, and "how-to's" for bringing the world to your classroom door. While by no means comprehensive, this list of Web links offers many good starting points for research and enrichment. Use keywords with the search function on each Web site to find specific topics. Many sites also offer tabs or pull-down menus for teachers, parents, and youth.

ANTIBULLYING AND COMMUNITY SAFETY

National Crime Prevention Council (www.ncpc.org) Presents resources for kids, teens, and parents, including materials related to ending bullying and identity theft.

Wisconsin Clearinghouse for Prevention Resources (wch.uhs.wisc.edu) Provides useful antibullying links.

CITIZENSHIP, COMMUNITY SERVICE, AND SERVICE-LEARNING

Corporation for National and Community Service (www.nationalservice.org) Provides resources for a variety of community service projects and age levels.

Kids Involved Doing Service (KIDS) Consortium (www.kidsconsortium.org) This nonprofit promotes civic involvement and citizenship in youth of all ages. The Web site features extensive service project ideas across subject areas and provides thoughtful Web resources. Teachers, administrators, and community partners will find useful ideas to collaborate effectively with students on solving community problems. Teachers can match projects to school curricula and state standards.

Learn and Serve America's National Service-Learning Clearinghouse (www.servicelearning.org/instant_info/kids_teens) Offers detailed materials for project ideas and readings for all kids and teens.

DISABILITY AWARENESS AND INCLUSIVENESS

Disability Is Natural (www.disabilityisnatural.com) Colorado author Kathie Snow's Web site focuses on her book *Disability is Natural,* which encourages new ways of thinking about kids and adults with disabilities.

Kids Together, Inc. (www.kidstogether.org) This volunteer organization promotes inclusiveness for all people, regardless of ability. It offers information and resources for children and adults with disabilities, including an extensive list of links to agencies and organizations that provide advocacy materials.

Partners in Policy Making (www.partnersinpolicymaking.com)
Focuses on the disability community. Features an extensive array of Web links to disability awareness topics such as activism, inclusion and community living, education, health care, self-determination, employment, family resources, and technology.

ENVIRONMENT

Clean Water Action (www.cleanwateraction.org)
Offers issue papers and publications about environmental action necessary for keeping the water supply safe.

Earthwatch Institute (www.earthwatch.org)
Includes environmental projects, curricula, and resources for teachers, youth, and families.

U.S. Environmental Impact Statements
(www.library.northwestern.edu/transportation)
An extensive national archive of environmental papers describing the anticipated effects of man-made physical changes on the environment.

U.S. Environmental Protection Agency (www.epa.gov/epaoswer/education)
This Web site features environmental awareness curricula for various age groups. Topics include "greenscaping," "green shopping," waste reduction, climate change, and environmental science projects.

GENERAL NEWS

BBC World Service (news.bbc.co.uk)
British Broadcasting Corporation's up-to-date world news source.

Canadian Broadcasting Corporation (www.cbc.ca/news)
Canadian and world news source.

National Public Radio (www.npr.org)
National and international radio news source with extensive links to topical news.

HEALTH/WORLD HEALTH

Kids Health (www.kidshealth.org)
The Nemours Foundation's Center for Children's Health Media sponsors Kids Health, a Web site that offers practical health-related information for parents, kids, and teens.

Morbidity and Mortality Weekly Report (www.cdc.gov/mmwr)
Offers extensive reports and summaries of worldwide health conditions and chronic and acute health concerns.

World Health Organization (www.who.int)
WHO directs and coordinates health concerns within the United Nations system and is responsible for providing leadership on global health matters. Features an A to Z listing of world health concerns.

Habitat for Humanity (www.habitat.org)
Offers information on providing safe and affordable housing around the world, as well as fact sheets and homeowner and volunteer stories.

Social Edge (www.socialedge.org)
Provides extensive information and links on homelessness, poverty, and human rights.

HUMAN RIGHTS

Children's Defense Fund (www.childrensdefense.org)
Provides extensive background materials on the status of children in the United States, including child health, nutrition, and living conditions.

Free the Children (www.freethechildren.com)
Web site features "Get Involved" resources to heighten awareness of child poverty and exploitation and offers specific information on starting your own campaign. Founded in 1995 by international child rights activist Craig Kielburger, winner of the Children's Nobel Prize and the Human Rights Award from the World Association of Non-Governmental Organizations.

Human Rights Campaign (www.hrc.org)
Provides background information on human rights issues related to gay, lesbian, bisexual, and transgender persons.

Human Rights Watch (www.hrw.org)
Nonprofit nongovernmental organization offers extensive background material on global human rights issues, including free downloadable reports.

MULTICULTURAL EDUCATION

University of Wisconsin Division of Cooperative Extension 4-H Resources (www.uwex.edu/ces/4h)
Provides experiential and multicultural education resources.

SOCIAL ACTIVISM AND SOCIAL ENTREPRENEURSHIP

Added Value (added-value.org)
Urban agriculture, youth leadership, and related issues are the focus of this Brooklyn-based organization.

Children, Youth and Families Education and Research Network (www.cyfernet.org)
A gateway to many, many links related to social activism for kids, teens, families, and educators.

Heifer Project (www.heifer.org)
Nonprofit organization devoted to ending hunger and creating sustainable communities. This Web site offers resources for both teachers and youth.

Peace Corps (www.peacecorps.gov)
This Web site offers lesson plans, stories, and newsletters focusing on world peace and sustainable development.

Taking It Global (www.takingitglobal.org)
A Toronto-based nonprofit organization that connects youth around the world and provides resources for getting involved in improving local and global communities.

Teaching Tolerance (www.tolerance.org)
Southern Poverty Law Center's Teaching Tolerance Web site offers many outstanding curriculum ideas for teaching youth and adults about tolerance, bias, and living in a diverse society.

What Kids Can Do (www.whatkidscando.org)
Nonprofit organization that supports youth activism. Features an exceptional collection of Web links to global education, citizenship, service-learning, justice, youth development, youth policy advocacy, youth media, and youth voting and political involvement resources.

YOUTH DEVELOPMENT

Forum for Youth Investment/Connect for Kids (www.connectforkids.org)
Offers materials related to child advocacy and policy development.

Helping America's Youth (www.helpingamericasyouth.gov)
Check out the Community Guide and Take Action tabs, with links to youth-adult partnerships, assessing a community's strengths, gathering census data, and finding youth programs linked to community risk factors.

The Innovation Center (www.theinnovationcenter.org)
Many links for community and youth development initiatives (sponsors At The Table, www.atthetable.org, a Web site for youth public policy advocacy).

National Youth Development Information Center (www.nydic.org)
Offers links to a wide range of teen advocacy information.

University of Arizona/National 4-H Council's Building Partnerships for Youth (msg.calsnet.arizona.edu/fcs)
Features a youth development curriculum, among many other resources.

Wisconsin Clearinghouse for Prevention Resources (wch.uhs.wisc.edu)
Provides many useful youth development links.

Notes

1. The discussion of Easter Island is based on (1) Michael Kiefer, "Fall of the Garden of Eden," *International Wildlife*, July-August (1989):38–43; (2) Terry L. Hunt and Carl P. Lipo, "Late Colonization of Easter Island," *Science* 311 (2006):1603–1606; and (3) Terry L. Hunt, "Rethinking Easter Island's Ecological Catastrophe," *Journal of Archaeological Science* 34 (2007):485–502.

2. The Associated Press, "Ah-Choo, Arizona No Longer Haven for Allergy Sufferers," *Corvallis (Oregon) Gazette-Times*, 25 March 1997.

3. The discussion of the Aswan Dam is based on (1) Chris Maser's personal experience; (2) C. J. George, "The Role of the Aswan Dam in Changing Fisheries of the South-Western Mediterranean," in *The Careless Technology*, ed. M. T. Farvar and J. P. Milton (New York: Natural History Press, 1972); and (3) James P. M. Syvitski, Charles J. Vörösmarty, Albert J. Kettner, and Pamela Green, "Impact of Humans on the Flux of Terrestrial Sediment to the Global Coastal Ocean," *Science* 308 (2005):376–380.

4. The discussion of the Bodélé depression is based on I. Koren, Y. Kaufman, R. Washington, M. Todd, Y. Rudich, J. Vanderlei Martins, and D. Rosenfeld, "The Bodélé Depression: A Single Spot in the Sahara That Provides Most of the Mineral Dust to the Amazon Forest," *Environmental Research Letters*, 1 (2006):1–5.

5. The discussion of rain forest biodiversity is based on Louise H. Emmons, "TropicalRain Forests: Why They Have So Many Species, and How We May Lose This Biodiversity Without Cutting a Single Tree," *Orion* 8 (1989):8–14.

6. Excerpted from *Step by Step! A Young Person's Guide to Positive Community Change* by The Mosaic Youth Center Board of Directors with Jennifer Griffin-Wiesner (Minneapolis: Search Institute, 2001).

Index

About the Authors

Jennifer Griffin-Wiesner is a youth development consultant and author specializing in working with young people and their communities to build a better world. Her most recent projects include consulting with youth-serving organizations on improving program quality, developing curricula for training and educating youth workers in best-practice strategies, facilitating youth-led community mapping, and working with teams of youth and adults to develop tools for strengthening mentoring relationships. She holds an M.Ed. in youth development leadership and is the author or co-author of many publications, including *Step by Step: A Young Person's Guide to Positive Community Change* and *The Journey of Community Change: A How-To Guide for Healthy Communities • Healthy Youth Initiatives.* You can learn more about Jennifer and her work at www.jengw.com.

Chris Maser is an author, international lecturer, and facilitator in resolving environmental conflict, creating vision statements, and working toward sustainable community development. He spent more than 25 years as a research scientist in natural history and ecology, working around the globe and with the U.S. Department of the Interior and Bureau of Land Management as a research ecologist and as a landscape ecologist with the Environmental Protection Agency. Chris has published 30 books, including his most recent, *Trees, Truffles, and Beasts: How Forests Function,* co-authored with Andrew W. Claridge and James M. Trappe. Chris holds an M.S. in zoology from Oregon State University. For more information about Chris and his work, visit www.chrismaser.com.

More Great Books from Search Institute Press

PROFESSIONAL DEVELOPMENT

A Quick-Start Guide to Building Assets in Your School
Moving from Incidental to Intentional
By Deborah Davis and Lisa Race

On top of budget cuts, changing curricula requirements, and dwindling instructional time, teachers and educational assistants are expected to "do more with less." *A Quick-Start Guide to Building Assets in Your School* helps education professionals do just that: make a more positive impact on students with less effort. Teachers can scan each segment separately for dozens of asset-building ideas to incorporate into their next group session. Each section offers reflection questions for teachers ("When do you remember having a voice in your own educational experience?"), as well as school-wide strategies to involve parents, students, and other school staff in creating healthy, caring classrooms.

$9.95; 28 pages; softcover; 8 1/2" x 11"

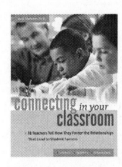

Connecting in Your Classroom
18 Teachers Tell How They Foster the Relationships That Lead to Student Success
by Neal Starkman, Ph.D.

If you want to be remembered as the best teacher they ever had, it takes more than knowing your subject and teaching it well. Teachers who excel—the ones who are remembered and whose students come back to visit them year after year—also make strong, empowering connections with their students. In *Connecting In Your Classroom*, both the humanity and professional secrets of "gold star" K–12 teachers are revealed. The principles of TEACH—trust, engagement, asset building, care, and hard work—are the basis of this inspirational guide to improving teacher-student relationships. Eighteen teachers from across the country share their secrets of how to encourage responsibility, empathy, and hard work—qualities that lead to academic and personal achievement—in their everyday interactions with students. Rooted in the Developmental Assets approach, these narratives inspire concrete, commonsensical, and positive experiences and qualities essential to raising successful young people.

$12.95; 144 pages; softcover; 7" x 9"

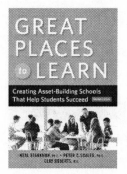

Great Places to Learn
Creating Asset-Building Schools That Help Students Succeed, Second Edition
by Neal Starkman, Ph.D., Peter C. Scales, Ph.D., and Clay Roberts

This foundational book is a powerful, positive guide to infusing Developmental Assets into any school community. From building awareness to sustaining system-wide changes, *Great Places to Learn* offers a step-by-step outline to guide school administrators, principals, and teachers through the process of integrating assets into their school while firsthand accounts provide the creative inspiration to adapt the concept to any situation. Includes a CD-ROM with reproducible handouts, charts, action lists, and assessment tools for everyone—from principals to bus drivers; Search Institute's latest survey data; and discussions on bullying, school violence, and the effect of the No Child Left Behind Act on school communities.

$34.95; 216 pages; softcover (includes CD-ROM); 7" x 10"

Powerful Teaching
Developmental Assets in Curriculum and Instruction
Edited by Judy Taccogna, Ph.D.

Powerful Teaching deals with the core of everyday classroom teaching and learning, and shows education professionals how to infuse Developmental Assets into existing curriculum and instruction without starting a new program. The book highlights research-based instructional strategies that teachers can use and adapt to their particular needs, plus real examples in Language Arts, Social Studies, Mathematics, Science, Health Education, and Visual Arts. *Powerful Teaching* allows teachers to focus on individual needs and foster the academic, social, and emotional growth of the whole student.

$42.95; 304 pages; softcover; 8 1/2" x 11"

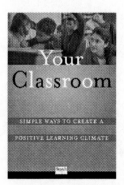

Your Classroom
Simple Ways to Create a Positive Learning Climate
by Marilyn Peplau

Looking for a simple tool to share the asset message with teachers? This booklet introduces the Developmental Assets and encourages teachers to foster growth of the eight asset categories in their students through day-to-day classroom interactions. It offers tips to build asset-rich relationships with young people, create a positive classroom environment, and infuse assets into their existing practices. Teachers can also use *Your Classroom* in advisory or other relationship-building roles—even in parent interactions.

$14.95; 24 pages, booklet (pack of 20); 5 1/2" x 8 1/2"

Best of Building Assets Together

Favorite Group Activities That Help Youth Succeed

Edited by Jolene Roehlkepartain

This indispensable resource presents over 150 "best of the best" activities that will energize and inspire any group of young people ages 12 to 18. Grounded in Search Institute's 40 Developmental Assets framework, these games and projects explore such topics as family communication, school climate, leadership, peer relationships, service-learning, diversity, and self-esteem. The book includes more than 25 new activities, as well as dozens of updated favorites, and focuses on empowering young people to discover their strengths. Includes real-world tips from educators and youth providers and a CD-ROM with over 50 reproducible handouts in English and Spanish.

$34.95; 160 pages; softcover (includes CD-ROM); 8 1/2" x 11"

Conversations on the Go

Clever Questions to Keep Teens and Grown-Ups Talking

by Mary Ackerman

Looking for a fun way to encourage family and other youth-adult conversations? *Conversations on the Go* is bound to get you talking. The book is filled with intriguing questions, guaranteed to stretch the imagination and bring out individual personalities. Adults and young people can take turns asking questions such as "If you were the smartest person in the world, what would you use your intelligence to do?" and "What does integrity mean to you?" and "If you could take the next year off, what would you do?" This stimulating, go-anywhere book gives teens and adults a chance to find out what the other thinks about questions both big and small.

$9.95; 100 pages; softcover; 5 1/2" x 5 1/2"

Great Group Games

175 Boredom-Busting, Zero-Prep Team Builders for All Ages

by Susan Ragsdale and Ann Saylor

Great Group Games offers 175 enjoyable games and activities that will gently disband group-busting cliques, help newcomers feel welcome, and turn your participants into friends who can count on each other. Authors Ragsdale and Saylor, experienced trainers and youth development leaders, have compiled games that are perfect for classrooms, retreats, workshops, and groups on the go. Each game includes details on timing, supplies, set-up, suggested group size, game tips, and reflection questions. Best of all, the games are far from mindless. "Tiny Teach," "Common Ground," and "The Winding Road" will really make your group members think. These low-prep activities work for small or large groups and can be done anywhere. You'll make every moment meaningful and every game great!

$16.95; 228 pages; softcover; 6" x 9"

Ideas That Cook

Activities for Asset Builders in School Communities
by Neal Starkman

Just as reading a great recipe can conjure up visions of a great meal, so too can this collection of great real-life activities inspire teachers and youth workers to "cook up" lasting good results with kids. Seventy-eight inventive activity recipes will get everyone's creative juices flowing.

$26.95; 168 pages; softcover; 8 1/2" x 11"

Engage Every Parent!

Empowering Families to Sign On, Show Up, and Make a Difference
by Nancy Tellett-Royce

Looking for sure-fire ways to get parents involved and engaged with their child's school, youth program, clubs, or athletic team? This book builds on research that shows just how important parent engagement really is. It offers "how-to" advice in the form of stories and examples of "best practices" in parent engagement, as well as handouts and other tools for interacting directly with parents. Topics include encouraging parents to show up, communicating about discipline issues, recruiting parent volunteers, reaching out to parents in impoverished communities, helping parents and caregivers remain engaged and feeling involved even when they work full-time, and communicating with parents through a variety of methods. Includes ice-breakers and activities for family and parent gatherings, talking points for calling or meeting with parents, and reproducible handouts for parents.

$29.95; 128 pages; softcover; 8 1/2" x 11"

Make a World of Difference

50 Asset-Building Activities to Help Teens Explore Diversity
by Dawn C. Oparah

A wide range of cultural competence is addressed in this creative resource for raising diversity awareness in teenagers. With a comprehensive approach that incorporates a variety of learning styles and skill levels, the three sections include personal-awareness activities for those with little exposure to diversity issues, a section for building cultural awareness around a particular topic, and practice activities for trying out new relationship-building methods. Each activity invites participants to examine their attitudes and behaviors about diversity and make the lesson tangible with group discussion. More than 20 reproducible activity sheets and scripts provide group leaders with hands-on tools and ready-to-use lesson plans, and a section on facilitation techniques helps program leaders guide sensitive discussions.

$26.95; 112 pages; softcover; 8.5" x 11"

Pass It On at School
Activity Handouts for Creating Caring Schools
by Jeanne Engelmann

Schools where students feel valued, supported, and cared for are the best places to learn. This activity-based resource equips everyone in the school community— teachers, students, administrators, cafeteria workers, parents, custodial staff, coaches, bus drivers, and others—with ready-to-use tip sheets and handouts to create change for the better by building Developmental Assets. The handouts are grouped by locations for asset building—in the classroom, cafeteria, locker room, nurse's office, in meetings, and more! It includes adaptable asset-building tips and ideas, engaging activities, and ideas for integrating Developmental Assets into your everyday efforts.

$24.95; 208 pages; softcover; 8 1/2" x 11"

Safe Places to Learn
21 Lessons to Help Students Promote a Caring School Climate
by Paul Sulley

The lessons in *Safe Places to Learn* challenge students to make their school a place where all students feel supported, accepted, and focused on classes, friendship, and fun activities. As a result, school becomes a warmer, safer place for all—teachers, staff, and students. *Safe Places to Learn* offers teachers, counselors, and other caring adults 21 lessons that challenge students in grades 6–12 to change attitudes and behaviors that perpetuate meanness. Students learn to promote kindness, respect, and caring while discouraging gossip, teasing, bullying, exclusion, and violence. They'll know how to effectively stop meanness when they see it—and do it in a respectful, caring way toward both the victim and the bully. Includes CD-ROM with reproducible handouts.

$29.95; 112 pages; softcover (includes CD-ROM); 8 1/2" x 11"

Taking It to the Next Level
Making Your Life What You Want It to Be
by Kathryn L. Hong

A booklet created just for teens and young adolescents, *Take It to The Next Level* helps young people focus on their successes, explore what they really want and how to get it, and celebrate their efforts and accomplishments. Filled with activities and journal topics, this booklet guides young people through the journey of adolescence from a Developmental Asset approach. A companion booklet to Search Institute's *Me @ My Best*, an introductory booklet on Developmental Assets for teens, *Take It to The Next Level* offers young people a chance to take the assets deeper by offering an opportunity for additional self-exploration and action.

$15.95; 20 pages, booklet (pack of 20); 5 1/2" x 8 1/2"

2712
Gift